Boomer Dad's
BOOK OF UNSOLICITED ADVICE

Boomer Dad's
Book of Unsolicited Advice

A Survival Guide

by
Hank Wohltjen

ISBN 979-8-218-05598-1

Cover design by ValentinaG
Book and ebook design by Booknook.biz

Contents

CHAPTER 9. SOME CLOSING THOUGHTS 141

BIBLIOGRAPHY 153

INTRODUCTION

While writing this book, I imagined overhearing this blistering critique: "How arrogant can someone be? Imagine, making suggestions to total strangers about how to live their life! Let me get this right: This is a book of advice from a geezer who probably doesn't even know what's real going on today. Yeah, this will be a great read. *Not.*"

I've been told that some folks would rather moonwalk barefoot on a smokin' hot Benihana grill than take advice from a baby boomer. It is absolutely true that most folks don't like unsolicited advice. Some psychologists say that giving unsolicited advice is a form of abuse, and those forcing it on others have a patronizing superiority complex. Maybe I'm different, but I have always been receptive to it. When another person offers me advice, it affirms that they are paying attention to me, and that they care enough to extend a helping hand. I sometimes ignore the advice, but I am always grateful for the helpful gesture.

This book is a primer of helpful advice originally written for my kids and grandkids, but which is relevant *to any young adult trying to navigate modern life*. The aim is to provide them with basic information on a broad range of subjects that they weren't necessarily taught in school. Consider it a version of the *Boy Scout Handbook* that can serve as a quick guide to surviving the complicated "jungle" that is modern life.

I feel confident in the advice I'm giving since I am a geezer with a lot of first-hand knowledge of the stuff written here. This book draws from a deep well of experiences. Now in my eighth decade, I've been a struggling student, an impoverished teacher, an engineer, a scientist, an inventor, an aviator, an entrepreneur, an investor, a CEO, a manager, a husband and a father. I've worked in small businesses, large businesses, government and academe. These collective experiences have exposed me to many different types of challenges and many different types of people. This book is my attempt to distill the important lessons of my personal experiences during these eight decades into a form that can be easily absorbed by others.

Transparently, some sections of this work do put me at the risk of being accused of *ultracrepidarianism* (the habit of giving opinions and advice on matters outside of one's knowledge or competence.—**ultracrepidarian**, *n., adj.*). I accept the risk and have walked that line carefully. Please trust that I will eschew obfuscation.

Lastly, I've organized the sections of this book are organized like a box-of-chocolates. Enjoy them in any order that suits your fancy, but here is how they are organized for publication:

Chapter 1 discusses you can best navigate on the road to life success—however you deem that success—by encouraging you to uncover and abide what are your core values. This takes work, and the work starts by **developing yourself.**

Chapter 2 focuses on those personal traits that will give you a powerful advantage when you engage with other people.

The work continues by developing an understanding of some of the quirks of human behavior. **Chapter 3** focuses on the weird world that we live in and tries to help you identify and avoid some traps that are waiting for you.

Chapter 4 offers cautionary advice on the hazards we face from internet connectivity and our long history of failure to consider the sustainability of our planet.

Chapter 5 reflects on the social interactions that accompany our daily lives and offers suggestions for developing skills that will allow you to enjoy life to the fullest.

Chapter 6 focuses on preparedness. There are many hazards to be considered: super-volcanoes, nuclear fallout, global pandemics, etc. (Yeah, some bad sh*t.) Read this and be ready.

Chapter 7 discusses some basics about jobs; suggestions on the skills required and how to get hired.

A lot of folks give serious thought to starting a business. If you're one of them, **Chapter 8** walks you through some of the ins-and-outs.

Chapter 9 enshrines the ramblings of an old geezer on random subjects.

Onward and upward to a good life!

ACKNOWLEDGEMENTS

Before you begin reading my unsolicited advice (and hopefully taking some of it), I must acknowledge some of those inspirational people who, often through unsolicited advice, taught me many of the lessons that are shared here:

My wonderful parents (Henry & Elizabeth), whose example of self-sacrifice helped me to form many of my core values. Being born into their loving family was better than winning the lottery.

Sharon, my lovely partner for more than 45 years and a distinguished university professor whose wit and intellect has enlightened me on so many topics and made me a better man.

My daughters Hannah, Sophie and Maggie. These exceptional women make the world a better place and make me very optimistic about the future.

Mr. Tom Whalen (R.I.P.). Once the Scoutmaster of Boy Scout Troop 25, he taught me about being prepared and how to remain calm in the face of chaos. He also gave me a deeply appreciated "scholarship" gift to attend summer camp when I was 12.

Brother Edward Lopez (R.I.P.), who opened my eyes to the exciting world of chemistry.

Brother John Flynn (R.I.P), who turned me on to physics, helped me get a ham radio license, and took me and several other radio nerds shopping for old surplus radio parts on Canal St. in NYC.

Fr. Robert Gannon (R.I.P), who prodded me to get my college applications submitted correctly and on time. He also arranged the scholarship that allowed me to go to college.

Prof. Nan Loh Yang, who gave me a research job at City University of New York (CUNY) when I was broke and who persuaded me to go to graduate school instead of becoming a bartender.

Mr. Steve "Cornfield" Carr, my first flight instructor who taught me most of what I know about unintentional spins, aerobatics and dead-stick landings.

Mr. Lou Chinal, who taught me the value of having a properly packed parachute when exiting airplanes in-flight.

Prof. Raymond Dessy (R.I.P.), who served as my graduate advisor at Virginia Tech and guided me to an incredible job at IBM Research.

Mr. Peter Vettiger, who was my colleague, guardian, language instructor and best man at my wedding when we worked at IBM Research Zurich making superconducting computer chips.

Dr. Arthur Snow, a friend and long-time scientific colleague from CUNY and the U.S. Naval Research Laboratory (NRL). His breadth and depth of scientific knowledge was always an inspiration to me., and I remain grateful for his several failed attempts to teach me how to surf.

Dr. Neldon Jarvis (R.I.P), an exemplary manager and human being who hired me at NRL and later became a friend, scientific colleague and business partner.

ACKNOWLEDGEMENTS

Mr. Felix Hampton (R.I.P), who spent years teaching me most of what I know about leadership, ethical business management and US government contract cost accounting.

I also need to acknowledge my personal board-of-directors who I've known since high school. These folks have kindly provided me with valuable unsolicited advice for almost 60 years:

Gerard Andrews
Eugene Borrelli
Louis Chinal
Kevin Daly
Dr. Christopher Gostout
Hon. Raymond Kennedy
Peter Marzano
Steven Nichols
William Randle
Robert Semler, Esq.
George Snyder, Esq.

I'd like to thank my friends, Lynette and Steve Haggbloom, Max Mendel and Chris Gostout for their adventurous nature and willingness to accompany me to the Alternative Energy Zone camp at Burning Man.

Finally I must express my sincere appreciation to editor Elizabeth Zack who took the original mish-mash of jibberish in my original manuscript and shaped it into the coherent masterpiece that you have before you.

Chapter 1.

NAVIGATE LIFE'S TWISTING ROAD: FIND YOUR COMPASS

Knowing your core values and making choices and decisions that are consistent with those values can serve as the compass that will guide you to future success.

OK, there's good news, and there's bad news. The good news is that you are living at an amazing time in human history. You have more opportunities than most humans of the past could ever imagine. You are very likely to enjoy a healthier life and a greater affluence than the vast majority of humans who walked on this planet before you.

The bad news is that this world is very complicated, treacherous and full of traps. The world is changing fast. There is evil out there. How can you become a positive force in this world? How can you safely find your way through the jungle?

This book offers some advice to help you navigate the twisting, turning, sometimes washed-out road of life. In it, I share observations and perspectives with you. Much of what is presented here is based on the premise that **the trajectory of our lives is largely determined by the decisions that we make.** Each decision that we make sets us on a path, and prudent choices and decisions can lead us to a good life.

Here is a two-step process to help you find a compass that will lead you to the right life path.

Step #1: Understand the Importance of Your Decisions

We all know happy people, sad people, successful people and unsuccessful people. What makes the difference? We walk on the same planet, breathe the same air and share more than 99% of our genes with others. Yet **every one of us makes our own personal decisions that ultimately lead us to our fate.** Bad decisions can lead us to squander our resources, miss opportunities and cause us to suffer abusive relationships. So preparing ourselves to make good decisions should be a high priority. Effective decision-making is critically important to our success.

Making good decisions requires us to develop personality traits that make us self-confident, knowledgeable and calm. We need to recognize the sometimes-unpredictable behavior of those around us and develop social skills that will give us the tools to navigate that weirdness and still enjoy life to the fullest.

Strong decision-making that brings us where we want to go is also about **learning to accurately assess the risks that we might face so that we can avoid taking dumb risks.**

Step #2: Establish Your Core Values

How do we prepare ourselves to make good decisions? **The preparation begins with introspection:** It requires that we figure out what is really important to us. Reflecting on these priorities over a period of time will ultimately reveal a set of core values that provide the bedrock for our personal decision-making.

Finding our core values can be harder to do than we might think. It is a quest that often continues throughout our lives, and it is essential to our personal decision-making process. Let me explain.

Life presents us with many controversial situations where it is not immediately clear what we should do or what position we should take. I admire individuals who, when confronted with a complex, uncomfortable situation, are able to respond quickly, thoughtfully and decisively. These folks invariably knew their core values and so could deftly apply them to the situation at hand.

Like most of us, I started developing my core values from things that I was taught at home and in school as a young child. Joining the Boy Scouts of America was a strong influence on the core values that I came to accept. My troop was led by men of integrity, generosity and compassion. Being in the Boy Scouts taught me the importance of being prepared and how to find my way through the woods. It also taught me about our duty to God, country, family, and those in need. The Boy Scouts contributed greatly to the core values I still use to navigate daily life.

The Road to Successful Navigation

Over the ages, navigators have always had one thing in common: the need for stable reference points. Early navigators used landmarks like mountains and streams to guide their journeys. As humans became more experienced at understanding the natural world around them, they began using the stars as guides, until the discovery of the magnetic compass that gave man a reference point that revolutionized navigation.

Those people who developed strong navigating skills went on to rule the world. They knew where they wanted to go and had the means to figure out a path to their destination.

Author and mathematician Lewis Carroll famously said, *"If you don't know where you're going, any road will get you there."* When you have well-established core-value reference points, it enables you to quickly find the road to a destination that is true to **your** values.

Staying True

Having well-established values can help us recognize when we are about to lose our way and become hypocrites, professing one thing but doing another. It clarifies the line that divides expedient positions of the moment from positions that are less convenient but truer to our core values.

Today our society is immersed in hypocrisy; examples abound. Some people say they are "pro-life." Just like any other core value, it needs to be sincerely held. It's fine to be "pro-life," but it seems like hypocrisy if pro-lifers also support the death penalty, or do not vigorously support programs for single mothers, improved daycare alternatives and early childhood education.

Other people demonstrate hypocrisy when they proclaim their support of free speech, yet then try to "cancel" those voices expressing ideas with which they disagree. So as you can see, the choice of your "core-values" can be tricky if you don't want to be a hypocrite. **When your actions mirror your values then you are not a hypocrite.**

Core values need to be clearly articulated and understood so that we better understand and make the right choices for what we support and how we act today and in the future. Here are some of the core-values I try to uphold that I'd like to offer for your consideration as you embark on the path to exploring and discovering your own core values.

Consider These Five Critical Core Values

Core Value #1: As an American, embrace the radical idea expressed in the Declaration of Independence that **"all men are created equal."** Embrace it knowing that it applies to people of all races, genders and creeds. This critical core value is not always easy to abide.

Core Value #2: As a human being, embrace the notion that **every human being deserves respect.** You don't have to like everyone, but you do need to respect everyone's right to "life, liberty and the pursuit of happiness."
Having respect for our fellow human beings is a critical core value. Recognize that it is not always easy to offer this respect.

Core Value #3: Commit yourself to **integrity**. Recognize that your word is your bond. Follow the rules, and avoid being deceitful. Accept that doing this is not always the easy path.

Core Value #4: Commit yourself to **celebration and thanksgiving.** Understand that every day is a gift. Live each day deliberately and celebrate at every opportunity. Be quick to give thanks for the kindness of others and the good things that come your way.

Core Value #5: Commit yourself to **preparedness.** Recognize your obligation to develop yourself mentally, physically, financially and spiritually so that you can be independent and able to serve and assist others.

Once you have developed a set of core values that ring true to you, and have them clearly established in your mind, then it will be easier for you to prioritize the many decisions that you will face. For decisions to be useful, we must act upon them. Action takes ability. Do you have what it takes for decisive actions? Chapter 2 describes personality traits that will give you a powerful advantage when you engage with other people.

Chapter 2.

THE RIGHT STUFF: BECOME READY FOR THE JOURNEY

Some people seem to have all the "right stuff." They are active and fun to be with and seem able to achieve their ambitions with ease. While it is possible to be naturally gifted in these areas, most of us need to consciously develop the traits described in the pages of this chapter.

Positive Attitude

Maintaining a positive attitude is the conscious act of engaging our imaginations to find hope in our lives.

It's hard to overestimate the importance of maintaining a positive attitude. We cannot survive a serious illness without a positive attitude, and for many, dealing with the recent pandemic was difficult due to fear and a negative mindset. Without a positive attitude, dealing with the daily grind can lead to despair.

The key to a positive attitude is *hope*. The key to hope is our imagination. **Our imagination is the tool that allows us to see paths away from our troubles.**

We are generally unable to do things that we believe cannot be done. So for instance:

- There is no way that pole-vaulters can fling their bodies over the bar if they don't believe that they can do it.
- If you believe that you are going to fail at something, then you probably will.

If you don't think that you can do something that really needs to be done, then you **need to assume a positive attitude, engage your imagination, and figure out how you CAN do it.**

Repeat to yourself a few times with conviction, "Failure is not an option," and then move on to figure something out. **Be an optimist... but also make a realistic plan.**

Another aspect of maintaining a positive attitude is being receptive to other people's ideas. It is easy to just say "no" when someone offers a new idea or a different plan.

Don't be a "Dr. NO". If the plan doesn't generate your immediate enthusiasm, then at least offer to think about it (unless, of, course the "great new idea" is to film your mid-air crash on a snowboard for the next Jackass movie. Just say "no" to that.)

Also, just say "no" to any plan of yours that begins with the words, "Hold my beer...".

Respect for All People

Always try to put yourself in the other guy's shoes. It might change the way you walk.

You deserve respect. So do all other people.

Showing respect to other people is not always easy, and often requires conscious action to do it. Respect must be offered regardless of gender, race, religious beliefs, political beliefs, age, or sexual orientation. You should never treat another person as inferior.

The amount of respect we hold for others is revealed on a regular basis when we're in public interacting with people whose job it is to serve us (e.g., waiters in a restaurant, baggage handlers, taxi drivers, and so forth). Do we speak to them respectfully and tip appropriately? If not, we need to adjust our behavior.

For example, consider treating a homeless person with the same respect as you would show to a well-dressed celebrity, for that doesn't always come naturally. **It is an act of grace to show respect to others first, even if you think they don't deserve it.**

But if we are to be true Americans, then we need to diligently respect the right of our fellow human beings to freely live the life that they choose in the way that they choose (within the constraints imposed by our laws, of course). America was started by people from around the world who were seeking tolerance to practice their chosen interests and religions.

The American Declaration of Independence stated: "We hold these truths to be self-evident, that all men are created equal, that they are endowed by their Creator with certain unalienable Rights, that among these are Life, Liberty and the pursuit of Happiness." It is still our duty today, and in the future, to carry on this tradition of American tolerance by respecting all people.

Respecting people, and their rights to life, liberty and the pursuit of happiness, is not the same as liking them. You don't have to like anybody, but you've got to acknowledge their equal rights to the privileges and opportunities that you enjoy.

It is a reality that some people are frightened by others who aren't like them. It is a fear that must be overcome. Different people make the world a more interesting place, but it also helps to become aware that, in spite of superficial differences, **all people have much more in common than those differences suggest. Learn to celebrate diversity.**

Also, never forget that it is as important **for you to have self-respect** as it is for you to respect others.

Honesty and Integrity

It is critical to understand that your word must be your bond.

If you say that you're going to do something, then commit yourself to doing what you said you'd do. If you're uncertain of your ability to do something, then just say so. **The trust that you will earn by being consistently honest with others will be among the most valuable things that you possess.**

Try to be fair in all transactions. Avoid being deceitful. Pay your bills on time. Don't take unfair advantage of others. When in doubt, do the right thing.

When we've made mistakes, honesty and integrity demand that we attempt to repair the damage. **Meaningful apologies contain three key things: regret, responsibility and remedies.** If you really want to apologize for something that you've done wrong, then consider doing the following:

1) Tell the other person that you are sorry for what happened.
2) Admit that you were wrong and that you now understand how they were hurt by your actions.
3) Tell them what you are going to do to prevent this from happening again.

Such apologies take honesty, integrity and courage. It is important to realize that there are a lot of folks in the world who can never bring themselves to apologize for their misdeeds. Many can't handle the shame of admitting that they were wrong. Others simply choose to deny that any meaningful harm was done, while other people simply cannot accept that they are at fault and try to blame someone else. Such folks never get to enjoy the transformative feeling of forgiveness that offering an apology can bring.

Don't be afraid to show your honesty and integrity. Apologize when it's appropriate and hope for forgiveness.

Fearlessness and Self-Confidence

Don't just accept your fear. Do something about it.

So many of us live in fear. Fear of being hurt. Fear of not having enough money. Fear of not being liked by others. Fear of bugs. Fear of not being good enough. Fear of the unknown. The list goes on. We must take conscious steps to examine our fears and come up with a plan to increase our self-confidence so that our fears will be diminished. **Fear is a big obstacle to living life to the fullest.**

Becoming fearless can be tough to do in the current world in which we live. Horrible disasters and personal tragedies are broadcast to us instantly and constantly from around the world. Politicians want us to be afraid so that we'll vote for their protective policies. Insurance companies want us to worry about potential disasters so that we'll buy more insurance. It is a shame that our leaders don't spend more time encouraging us NOT to be afraid.

Our fears prevent us from enjoying the full range of life's experiences. We should be afraid of some things, like playing with poisonous snakes and wild animals, skiing in avalanche zones, standing under a tree in a lightning storm, and putting gasoline on the barbeque grill. Likewise, there are some things that we should **not** be afraid of, like speaking up against injustice, learning how to dance, travelling to someplace new, helping others in need, speaking in front of a group, and trying new foods.

Where do we get the self-confidence to be fearless? We get it by **identifying what we're afraid of and figuring out a way to put ourselves into a position that will reduce the fear.** For example, if we're worried about not having enough money, then we come up with a budget and stick-to-it. If we don't have enough money coming in to meet the budget, then we figure out what kind of job that we need to meet the budget. If we don't qualify for that kind of job, then what kind of training do we need to get the job?

Don't just accept your fear. Do something about it. Work on your list of fears one at a time and whittle it down so that you'll be ready to enjoy the fullness of life. Don't let fear keep you from achieving your dreams.

The Courage to Speak Out

Enabling the bad behavior of others through our silence makes us complicit in that bad behavior.

Courage is defined by Merriam-Webster as, "the mental or moral strength to resist opposition, danger or hardship. It implies firmness of mind and will in the face of danger or extreme difficulty."

We all aspire to be courageous, but most of us don't always achieve it when put to the test. It's true our courage can be tested in extreme events (like wars or dangerous confrontations), but these events are rare. Rather, our courage is tested on a regular basis when we see something significant that is wrong and needs a voice to help "right the wrong." **If we remain silent then we've not shown courage. Ignoring bad behavior simply enables it in the future.**

When conflict arises that we cannot avoid, we should examine our core values and pick a side, then find the courage to stand up and resist the opposition. Attending public demonstrations and rallies requires courage, but demonstrations are an essential part of how our American democracy works.

When confronted with a public demonstration, some of us wish that the police would just make the demonstrators go away, not caring if the issue behind the demonstration is justified or not. Fortunately, other citizens try to learn about the issues and decide whether they should join the demonstration.

Our country needs more people who have an open mind and the willingness to actively support their convictions. At the very least, as citizens we need to vote and support those things that we think are right and oppose those things that we think are wrong.

Calmness Under Pressure

In any crisis situation it is of utmost importance to quickly recognize that you are in a crisis situation.

When things are going to hell all around you, it can take skill and nerves of steel to remain calm. In situations like this, the single most important thing to understand is that panic will not help you in any way. You must remain calm and think things through.

Recognizing that you are in a crisis situation requires mental focus. This is not always easy to do; sometimes the situation is murky or difficult to understand. Failure to make a conscious determination that a crisis exists leads many folks to confusion, panic and bad decisions. Once you are consciously aware of the crisis on your hands, then you can deliberately put your mind in "crisis mode "and focus on dealing with the crisis.

Many parents experience a looming panic when their child receives a serious injury, such as a deep wound. In such a situation, it is best if they place their minds in crisis mode, remaining calm and focused. For instance, they may need to take a deep breath; go to their first-aid "ABC" training (i.e., "Airway", "Breathing", Circulation"); and stop their child's bleeding by applying pressure to the wound. Then they work on getting some medical help by calling 911 and/or proceeding to the emergency room, etc. If they panic or begin screaming hysterically when they first see their kid bleeding, then they're definitely not helping them.

Here is a Four-Step Crisis Course of Action to consider when there is a crisis presenting itself in your world:

Step #1)   Quickly decide if you are dealing with a crisis or not.
Step #2)   Identify the most serious problem with which you're dealing.
Step #3)   Figure out what resources/options are available to deal with that problem.
Step #4)   Begin pursuing the best option available.

It's a great course of action. If you panic in any life-threatening situations, then you or someone else could die. For example, some describe flying airplanes as "hours of boredom punctuated by moments of sheer terror." There are many things that can produce these "moments of sheer terror:" an engine failure, a cockpit fire, flying through a flock of birds, unexpected severe turbulence, or icing of the airplane. If the pilot panics in any of these situations, then they, and their passengers, could easily die. But if they stay calm, keep flying the airplane, and follow the proper procedures, you'll all probably fly another day.

Calmness under pressure becomes easier when we focus on those things that we can control. The most important thing to realize is that it is pointless to worry about things that we cannot control. What will be, will be. Worry should be limited to those things that we CAN influence.

When confronted with a worrisome situation, take a careful look at it and try to determine if there is anything that you can do about it. If it's clear that you can't, then accept it and don't spend your time worrying. Grief or sadness maybe warranted, but worry is not.

Stay cool. Stay calm.

Perseverance

Perseverance is the most important factor behind personal achievement.

You don't have to be the brightest person, or the best-looking, or the most talented. You just need **a desire to achieve some goal and the willingness to work at it until you achieve the goal.**

Implicit in the notion of being perseverant is the requirement that you have carefully studied your goal and you believe that it can be achieved. It would be crazy to persist in trying to achieve a goal that you did not believe was actually achievable.

Thomas Edison is a good role-model for perseverance. Some of his ruminations that have proven to be true in my experience include:

- *"Genius is one-percent inspiration and ninety-nine percent perspiration."*
- *"I have not failed. I've just found 10,000 ways that won't work."*
- *"Many of life's failures are people who did not realize how close they were to success when they gave up."*

Perseverance is a personality trait that separates the winners from the losers. It is the commitment that we make to see a task to completion. Usually, it just involves a bit more work than expected on some mission to which we've committed ourselves. It is often the case that we underestimate the amount of time that it takes to achieve a goal.

Giving up guarantees failure. A little bit of perseverance can often deliver success.

Everything in Moderation

Moderation is the force that keeps us from "flying off the rails" so that we are able to achieve exceptional things.

The notion of avoiding excess has been a basic concept in many cultures and religions for thousands of years. It is related to the critical need to find balance in our lives. It is applicable to every facet of our lives. For example:

- We should moderate what we eat and drink. Avoid the urge to gorge ourselves on sugary desserts. Eat a broad range of foods (not just Pringles, ice cream and kimchi). Don't waste our time on starvation diets. Have a glass of wine with dinner (but don't drink the whole bottle).
- Use our smartphone, but restrict its use when in the presence of people who might enjoy speaking to us face-to-face.
- Moderate our social networking habits. Try to spend more time in the presence of real-live people instead of an electronic device.

- Moderate our work habits. Leave time for family, friends, exercise and hobby interests. Don't accept any job that demands loyalty to the company be our highest priority.
- Moderate our leisure habits. Don't binge-watch the entire season of any TV show unless you've got the day-after free to catch up on your sleep.

I'd also argue that we should all aim to be moderates in our political views. Moderates are more inclined to listen to both sides of an argument. Moderates are less bound by ideology and better positioned to make the compromises needed to keep our democracy going forward.

Moderation should not be confused with mediocrity. Mediocrity is uninspired and unexceptional. Moderation is the force that can keep us from "flying off the rails" so that we are able to achieve exceptional things.

Be moderate. Be exceptional.

Carpe Diem

Live your life, conscious of every waking moment.

Carpe Diem is a Latin phrase that means "seize the day." It's an extraordinarily important idea. Life is short. So many people squander their lives gliding on autopilot from day to day without conscious aim or purpose. This is a tragedy!

Carpe diem exhorts us to live deliberately, to recognize that every day is a gift. It reminds us to open our eyes and ears, look and listen to what is going on around us in this moment, smell the roses, engage with other people, and try to make a difference, today and every day. Remember the past and plan for the future, but not ignore the moment we are living in right now. **Be in the moment.**

Meditation is a common path that some folks choose to "be in the moment." They calmly focus on what is going on here and now. Worries about the past or the future are irrelevant. The immediate environment is all that matters. Meditation is a popular path, but choose whatever works best for you. Take a walk outside at lunch. Gaze at the evening sky. Listen to the birds.

You only have one life, so don't be a robot. Live it to the fullest. Turn off your autopilot. Put your hands on the controls of your plane and be conscious of the gift you have today.

When you get up in the morning, look in the mirror and say, "Carpe Diem." Then do it.

Be Aware of the Situation

Avoid trouble by always paying attention to what's going on around you.

Different people pay attention to different things. This is one reason why people can have such different perceptions of the world around us. Some people actively listen to the sounds around them, observe details of things that they see, and actively analyze this information to determine if things are proceeding "normally." Others walk along with earphones in place and a little hand-held screen 12 inches from their nose, oblivious to their immediate environment. They are watching a funny YouTube video or text message. They could be in the path of a speeding bus but wouldn't know it. Or fall off the cliff or dock (yes, this has happened more than once, with not always a positive outcome).

The first person had "situational awareness." The second person did not. The lack of situational awareness is a leading cause of human accidents. **Situational awareness involves:**

1) Active observation of our environment
2) Comprehension of what is going on, and
3) A projection of what might change in the immediate future.

I learned situational awareness growing up in New York City at a time when street crime and muggings were common. Situational awareness was an essential survival skill to living in the city. It was important to listen to my "inner-voice." If I knew that I was in a sketchy neighborhood, turned the corner to walk down a street, and saw a group of young guys standing around (possibly waiting to harass a passerby), then the wise move was to skip that street and turn down the next one where the coast was clear.

I've found learning to fly is a great way to develop situational awareness skills. It's a world where imperfect machinery, unpredictable weather, immovable objects and human abilities (or lack thereof) all come together at the same time. Good pilots are able to "stay ahead" of the airplane. They have everything working: proper engine settings, proper heading, altitude and airspeed. They scan the instruments carefully looking for anomalies. They are able to focus on navigating to the next waypoint and figuring out which direction they're going to turn and how they're going to communicate their intentions to air traffic control, all while carrying on a conversation with a passenger and carefully keeping an eye out for deteriorating weather conditions. Maintaining situational awareness takes conscious effort.

It's very dangerous to "get behind" the airplane, or any other vehicle for that matter. When something distracts you, like an engine running rough, then it's easy to focus on that and forget to continue monitoring everything else. Losing situational awareness when flying is not good. Losing situational awareness when driving a car is not great either. Put down the phone or stop looking intently at the beautiful person walking down the sidewalk.

When driving, do you pay close attention to the road ahead? Are there any hazards on the road? Are there small children or animals near the road? Is it getting cold? Is the road near freezing? What is the condition of your tires? Is there a car trying to pass you? Is the guy you just cut-off really angry? (Does he have a gun?)

Situational awareness is a skill worth cultivating for everyday living. People with good situational awareness are much less likely to blindly walk into a bank while there's a robbery going on. They'd see the face masks on the robbers, recognize that it's not Halloween (or a COVID pandemic), and choose to go pick-up their dry-cleaning next door instead.

So, how about it? Do you have "the right stuff"? How's your attitude? Can you offer respect to all people? Are you honest? Do you have self-confidence? Do you have the courage to speak out? Are you calm under pressure? Are you perseverant? Can you moderate yourself and live consciously in the moment? If you are able to embrace and cultivate these personal traits, then you will be well prepared to make the good decisions that build the foundation for a good life.

Chapter 3.

HUMAN NATURE: UNDERSTANDING THE WEIRDOS AROUND US

It's not always easy to understand people. Two people can be standing side-by-side witnessing the same event and come away with very different views of what just happened. Things that seem completely obvious to you may not be obvious to someone else, and vice versa.

It is a mistake to assume that different people will process information in the same way, and the recent COVID-19 pandemic serves as an example of this. It seemed paradoxical to me for anyone to conclude that it was OK not to wear a mask, or not get vaccinated during a raging global pandemic that was killing millions of people. Others saw the situation differently.

The root cause of this COVID-19 vaccination decision paradox is centered on the beliefs that we hold. Some of us believe that the established experts on infectious disease (e.g., the Centers for Disease Control (CDC) or the National Institutes of Health (NIH)) are the best source of information regarding infectious disease. This group believes that CDC information has been peer-reviewed by the scientific community and that the scientific method, though not perfect, is the best tool that mankind has to define objective facts. The group believes in the integrity of the CDC and its scientific experts, and they choose to believe the recommendations that they offer.

On the other hand, some of us are skeptical of the integrity of the CDC "experts," choosing instead to believe that their "objective science" is biased and their messaging politically driven. This group is willing to listen to, and believe, the critical voices of self-proclaimed experts who offer plausible condemnation of the expert CDC advice with (often un-verifiable) stories about how the CDC experts are lying or wrong. This group accepts information from unofficial sources because the stories align with their deeply held belief that everything is rigged by the estab-lished "experts".

The Power of Belief

Michael Shermer, a well-known American science writer and historian, and the executive director of The Skeptics Society, has written extensively on how humans form beliefs about the world. In his words:

> … Beliefs come first and explanations for beliefs follow. The brain is a belief engine. Using sensory data that flow in through the senses, the brain naturally begins to look for and find patterns, and then infuses those patterns with meaning, forming beliefs. Once beliefs are formed, the brain begins to look for and find confirmatory evidence in support of those beliefs, accelerating the process of reinforcing them, and round and round the process goes in a positive-feedback loop.

The strength with which so many of us hold our beliefs has made **beliefs the foundation for religions, cultures and all of our socially acceptable norms.** For instance, the "unalienable rights" described by the Declaration of Independence are not powered by any physical law, like gravity. The power behind the notion of unalienable rights comes from American's shared **belief** in the desirability and necessity of those rights. All religious faith comes from a conscious choice to believe in a divine entity. The power of our beliefs should not be underestimated, and so the formed beliefs that we hold are very, very, difficult for us to change.

Since beliefs are so powerful, we have a responsibility to ensure that our own beliefs are formed from carefully considered facts. It is generally accepted that the scientific method reveals "facts" about the world we live in. The scientific method relies on systematic observation, measurement and the formulation of appropriate hypotheses to explain the measurements. Review and reproduction of the observations and measurements by other interested scientists is key to accepting any hypothesis as "fact.". This process is known as "peer-review." The scientific method deals with documenting physically observable phenomena. It assumes that all "facts" are subject to modification when new information is available. It recognizes that its peer-reviewed conclusions may not be totally correct, but they are the best knowledge that we have.

We seem to be in a strange place today where some people are comfortable placing their personal beliefs on par with scientific fact. They then berate scientifically verifiable facts that don't align with their personal beliefs as "fake news" and hail claims from crackpots that do align with their beliefs as truth. These folks have come to a point where they regard their "beliefs" as "facts." This is nonsense. **The Cambridge English Dictionary** defines a "fact" as "something that is known to have happened or to exist, especially something for which proof exists, or about which there is information." Believing that the earth is flat does not make it a fact.

It is very difficult for other people to deal with the belief-based distortion of reality and self-deception. Perhaps the best we can do is to follow the old proverb, "You can lead a horse to water but you can't make it drink." Offer the facts, as you understand them, in the hope of persuading the misinformed person away from self-deception, but don't be surprised if your efforts are unsuccessful.

More importantly, **keep an open mind. Always be willing to consider the possibility that your beliefs on some issue could be wrong. Be curious and analytical in your thinking.**

Mysticism and Gut Feelings

The confusion between beliefs and facts has grown because the world has become extraordinarily complex and too difficult for most people to fully understand. For example, the conversion of mineral ore into a tin-can involves hundreds of steps and hundreds of technologies. Who understands any of this? Who has any detailed understanding of how cellular telephones or the internet actually work? How do you make a precision ball bearing? The details behind all of these things are mysterious and unintelligible to most people.

When we can't really explain where everything around us comes from or how it works, then it is mystical. De-mystifying the world takes a lot of lot of study and effort. This is a major goal of scientific research. A key virtue of the scientific method is that it causes our understanding of things to evolve continuously. Coming to truth is the ultimate goal, but the fallibility and limitation of our current knowledge is always recognized. No one is able to develop a functional understanding of how everything in our world works. We must be willing to accept that there are legitimate experts who do understand, at least partially, how some of these things work. Their advice is not always correct, but usually it is, and you'd be wise to heed their guidance on these subjects.

It has become popular for people to reject "expert" opinions and guidance when it doesn't align with their gut feelings. **Simply choosing to believe things because they align to your gut feelings is a lazy strategy that can quickly lead you away from the truth. There is no substitute for basing your beliefs on carefully considered facts obtained from reliable sources.**

Don't Be a Sucker for Conspiracy Theories

The COVID-19 pandemic was fertile ground for conspiracy theories. Governments, big-pharmaceutical companies, and billionaires were the "boogey-men." Some even believe that the vaccines contain microchip implants that can be used by Bill Gates to track people. Why? Some believe that COVID-19 was developed deliberately for population control. Really? And then there is the evil 5G cellphone network that is zapping our immune systems with radio waves and making us susceptible to the virus. Please wear your tin-foil hat! The list of nonsense goes on and on.

The same intellectual laziness that allows people to place their personal beliefs on par with proven facts also makes them susceptible to belief in conspiracy theories. When people are unable to bring understandable order into their world, they are inclined to seek order in the simple-minded explanations offered by conspiracy theories.

Is it possible that American astronauts never set foot on the moon and that the moon landing was filmed in a Hollywood studio? Some people believe that it was all a conspiracy by the US government to make it seem that the USA was beating the Russians in the space race. This is believable only to those who think that it is possible to have the tens of thousands of people involved in the space program lie about it. It's also only believable to folks who don't understand that the moon rocks contain unique mineral and chemical compositions that are not found in earth rocks and are easily identified in the lab.

Practicing scientists rarely waste their time with conspiracy theories. Upon examination, they often quickly recognize that the theory presents only a superficial "scientific" analysis, usually based on incorrect or unverifiable "facts." Rarely do conspiracy theorists cite any repeatable observations or peer-reviewed literature. They rely on pseudo-science that cannot withstand normal scientific scrutiny.

Conspiracy theorists are usually self-proclaimed skeptics and critical thinkers. They gravitate toward the central idea that a small group of elites control the world. They prefer the simple "boogey-man" explanation rather than grappling with the fact that the world is a very complex place with many uncoordinated forces acting to cause unexpected things to happen. Accordingly, most folks who believe conspiracy theories have great contempt for the elite boogey-men.

Conspiracy theories: Don't waste your time with that garbage.

Most People Are "Threes"

We experience many challenges when we need to work as a team. After many years of working with groups of contractors, committees, coworkers and friends, I began to realize that most people needed to be told something more than once before I could be sure that they knew what I was talking about. In fact, **most people needed to hear something new on three occasions before "the coin dropped" and the idea actually clicked in their minds.** Thus, the realization that "most people are threes" came about.

This phenomenon has nothing to do with intelligence. It has more to do with the attention that people are able give to those folks who are trying to communicate complex information, or who might not be expressing themselves clearly. Everyone has many things going on in their lives and our attention spans are limited.

I have come to understand that I am usually a "three" (and sometimes a "four") except when I'm dealing with folks who are on my team and with whom I share a common understanding of the mission and our individual personalities. With me these folks are "ones," since an idea only needs to be expressed once before everyone "gets it". Folks who are less frequent participants on the team are often "twos," and I learned that I had no reason to be impatient with them unless I had to explain myself more than twice. Those folks who were "threes", "fours" or even "fives" could be readily dealt with, without bringing me any frustration, since I knew that they were "fours" and I just needed to plan accordingly and keep track of how many times I had made my request to them. Thus, a difficult social interaction problem that gave me high blood pressure could be reduced to a simple, stress-free accounting problem.

Early in my scientific career I was given some unsolicited advice on how to make a good presentation at a meeting. In hindsight, I now realize that advice was based on the notion that "most people are threes" since I was told to:

1) tell 'em what you're going to tell 'em
2) tell 'em
3) tell 'em what you just told 'em.

The idea that most people are "threes" is extremely helpful when you're trying to pitch a new idea to a person or group. This allows you to realize that you have little chance of getting any meaningful response to your proposal if you only present it once. Most times, you need to hit them with the idea at least three times before you should expect anything to happen. Perseverance is required!

Good People and Bad People

Most people are good, but what about the bad people in the world? Folks like:

- Vladimir Putin has, with his oligarch friends, robbed much of Russia's wealth and started a senseless war, killing thousands of innocent people in Ukraine.
- Kim Jong-un enslaves North Korea with his weird ambitions.
- Xi Jinping has been methodically suppressing freedom in China and threatens to grab Taiwan against its will.

Such folks are really bad people, and autocratic murderers like this have always been around and will continue to exist. **It is necessary for good people around the world to oppose them whenever possible.**

On a day-to-day basis, we deal with a lot of people; fortunately, most people are good. Others have bad attitudes and are just a drag to be around. Some people are parasites who will take as much from you as they can. Some people are totally selfish and inconsiderate of others. And some people are just mean and evil. The best thing that you with these folks is to recognize that they're bad and simply avoid them. Stay as far away as you can. **It's OK to avoid them. They are poison.**

Yet there is no one walking on this planet who is 100% good or 100% bad. We have all done good things and bad things. **Our ambition should be to do as much good as possible and as little bad as possible.**

Good people and bad people are formed early in life. Getting your kids to develop core values about right and wrong at an early age (e.g., before the age of 3) is really important so that they'll make good decisions about choosing their friends when the time arises and you're not around.

How can you teach your good core values to toddlers? It's not as hard as you might think. **When the kids are showing good behavior, notice it, name it, and affirm that it's good.** Set simple, clearly defined rules and acknowledge their good behavior when they follow the rules. When someone else is exhibiting good behavior, then hold them up as a role model for the toddler. Little kids learn quickly.

Cancel Culture

Lately, a fad of "Cancel Culture" has emerged. Anyone can be subjected to total ostracism for some misdeed that is deemed outrageous by an internet-connected mob. Most folks being "cancelled" have achieved positions of power and notoriety from some form of popular or good work they've done. Reports of a heinous offense can trigger their "cancellation" by self-appointed critics.

Some will argue that "cancelling" is democratic in that it allows ordinary people to fight injustice and hold powerful people to account for their actions. Others say that cancel culture is nothing more than an internet-based lynch mob that usurps our legal protections under the law.

Cancel culture also manifests itself in the form of internet "trolling." This is a growing problem for young people where they can be effectively "cancelled" from social interactions with their group. This is brutal punishment for what are usually minor transgressions.

How much bad does a person need to do to be "cancelled"? Who decides this? If a person is shown to be bad, does that mean we should disregard the good that they've done? Many of the courageous signers of the Declaration of Independence owned slaves. Should they be cancelled? Is it OK to apply currently accepted moral norms to past behavior when the moral norms at that time were different?

Cancel culture is a slippery slope. Lynching a person's reputation on the internet is not a recipe for fairness. Serious misdeeds are already addressed by our laws and should be adjudicated in a fair hearing from both sides. It is better to leave these disputes to our courts and system of justice to resolve.

Chapter 4.

KNOW WHERE TROUBLE LURKS

It's often been said that "if something seems too good to be true then it probably is." This is very reliable advice. It is an excellent gauge that can alert you to potential trouble. Many things in the world are two-edged swords. They may be very useful, but also potentially dangerous. Let's think about some of them.

Beware the Internet

Many folks don't fully understand that all of the "free stuff" they've been getting on the internet is not really free. Sure, you don't need to pay money for it, but you're paying for it by giving away valuable private information. You're providing information about your interests and behavioral patterns to companies that use the information for marketing purposes. This is a blatant invasion of privacy and yet, most of us ignore that fact. If you go down this path, over a lifetime you will have revealed an incredible amount of information about yourself (some good, some bad, some inaccurate) that will be stored digitally forever.

Use the web cautiously. Don't leave a big digital footprint.

The "Internet-of-Things" (IoT) is making privacy matters much worse. Manufacturers of a vast array of products are enhancing the microprocessors that run their products with the ability to wirelessly connect to the internet. This will allow surveillance on an unprecedented scale. Your toaster will report everything that you toast. It will report if it was a slice of bread or a bagel. Your refrigerator will report how many times the door was opened. Your washing machine will report the settings (i.e., delicates, heavy soil, etc.) every time you do a load. Your TV will report what you watch and when you watch it. Your "smart" thermostats and security lighting will report what they're doing at all hours of the day. Your "Roomba" floor-cleaning robot will learn the layout of your rooms, where you have furniture, and the types of furniture you have, and it will report what it has learned. Alexa and Siri are always listening to you and sending information to who-knows-where to be used for who-knows-what.

"Artificial intelligence has gone too far. The refrigerator just texted that the dishwasher is talking behind my back."

CartoonStock.com

This is not science fiction. This is actually happening today. As people become more intoxicated by the notion of "smart" appliances, the surveillance will expand exponentially. Some people do like "smart" appliances because they do offer some conveniences, and they are unconcerned about any privacy issues. "Smart" appliances are touted for their ability to diagnose and report fault conditions, but these faults will immediately initiate unsolicited offers from the appliance manufacturer to fix the problem (for a charge, of course). **So "smart" appliances are not necessarily the smartest choice, especially if you value your privacy.**

The internet places us at constant risk of being seduced by the eye-candy and sensational garbage that abounds on this global bazaar. What is fiction? What is fact? Who knows? We drive our journey through the internet with mouse "clicks," and we reveal our interests by the amount of time we spend viewing the destination websites. We make choices when we pay attention to one thing and not another. The internet owes much of its existence to the fact that our attention, and associated choices, have enormous commercial value.

The internet absorbs a substantial percentage of the entire world's attention. It is the go-to place for everything: knowledge, entertainment, commerce, relationships, etc. Plus it absorbs so much of our unconscious attention that many of us don't even realize how it robs the attention that we are able to give to people living around us.

We are being manipulated by many of the "free" content-providers on the internet. Social media platforms are continuously pursuing ways to make the platform more appealing and addictive to their users. They want us to spend more time clicking through their sites. To the global advertising industry, our attention is the most valuable thing that is being bought and sold. Our website "clicks" reveal our behavioral patterns and preferences. This information can be sold to vendors who use it for targeted advertising. Who has access to this information? What are they going to do with it? How much do they actually know about us?

Be aware of this surveillance and consider not engaging extensively on social media. The information that you post can be used against you. Minimize your "digital-footprint" (i.e., traceable activities, communications and the "electronic breadcrumbs" that you leave when using the internet). Be aware that materials that you have deleted are likely to remain stored somewhere that you can't access.

"Son, it's time we talked about surveillance.

Other things you can do to reduce your risks of your privacy being invaded and information about you being stored and used for someone else's, or a business's, purposes:

- Consider using a browser (e.g., DuckDuckGo) that provides tracker-blocking and site-encryption. Some browsers offer extensions to provide these functions.
- Use separate email accounts for your personal activities and your professional, business-related activities.
- Avoid using your primary email address when creating accounts. Consider getting a free email account somewhere (e.g., Gmail) and using this as a "throw-away" when being forced to provide an email address to access some website that is likely to spam you.
- If you do use social media, then make sure that you don't over-share. Limit access to your posts to family, friends and trusted contacts.

Dealing with Information Pollution

The internet and worldwide web first appeared in 1990. Prior to that time, daily news flow was largely controlled by media outlets like radio, TV networks, newspapers and magazines. These organizations generally prided themselves on maintaining high standards of journalism. They reviewed the news of the day coming in from around the world and presented only those stories that were credible, verifiable and relevant to their audience. This system provided some censorship of information, but it shielded us from the vast sea of raw information. It also provided a foundation of common knowledge, based on stories that most of us could agree were factual.

The internet has changed all of that. Today everyone connected to the internet has a voice that can be heard by anyone else connected to the internet. There is very little oversight of the information being posted at rates currently approaching **100 million posts-per-minute**. Many of the posts are crazy opinions, some are fantasies, and others are just wrong or deliberately misleading.

The "free" internet information pipe has quickly turned into a massive sewer pipe. Hateful, lying voices are just as loud as peaceful, truthful voices. We are forced to navigate around piles of unwanted advertising, pornography, whack-o opinions, totally fake stories and inaccurate news. For most of us, this is simply noise that makes it difficult to find relevant, factual information. Drink the free internet Kool-Aid every day and you'll sink into the twilight zone.

Be skeptical of what you see and read on the internet. Rely on reputable information sources like the major national newspapers, magazines and professional/scientific journals. You might have to pay a subscription to get access to them, but it's worth it. Ignore the majority of health information that you see. Rely only on reputable information sources like the Mayo Clinic, WebMD, Health.gov and Medline. The best strategy is to limit your time exposing yourself to internet pollution. Beware the internet!

Don't Feed Trolls

And there's more! The internet has enabled some sociopathic people to go "trolling" by throwing provocative "bait" into the internet "water" with the hope that it will generate outraged responses. Trolling has been weaponized into a tool to antagonize, abuse and humiliate others.

Trolls are bullies and they hurt a lot of people. Young people have been known to commit suicide after being trolled. What can you do? The best ways to deal with trolls include:

- Disengaging. Don't feed the troll. Ignore them.
- Participate only in forums that are moderated and have enforced anti-trolling policies.
- Blocking, banning and reporting them.

EVOLUTION OF THE TROLL

CartoonStock.com

Prevent Identity Theft

Another great feature of the internet is that it provides thieves a really convenient way to rob us. All they need is a few key pieces of your information. Always be really careful whenever providing Social Security Number (SSN), date of birth and banking information (i.e., bank account numbers). The only folks with a routine legitimate need for this type of info (especially SSNs) are employers, government entities and banks.

Identity theft can be absolutely devastating. It can destroy your good credit rating, making it hard or impossible to get a loan or mortgage. Identity theft can result in you being hounded by debt collection agencies. And sometimes it is even necessary to engage an "identity theft attorney" to unwind the mess, which can take years to resolve.

Identity theft often starts with "phishing", when a thief sends you an email that looks like it's from a legitimate "official" organization and asks you for personal information. **Never provide personal information from your computer unless you are certain that you are connected to a legitimate entity.** If there is a request for personal information, then check the sender's address. If the address is not associated with the "official" organization, then trash it. Never click on anything unless you're confident that it is legit. Don't worry if you mistakenly trash a legitimate request; they'll send the request again if it's important and you haven't responded.

The same guidance applies to telephone solicitations. **Don't give them any information.** If you're polite enough not to just hang up on them, then tell them that you only consider written solicitations. If they ask for your address, then just say "good-bye."

On-line shopping and bill-paying is super convenient but exposes us to a significant risk. We routinely need to provide credit card information for purchases. These are easily stolen by unscrupulous people at the on-line companies from whom we're buying something. Fortunately, the credit card companies are quick to absorb the theft loss and to promptly cancel the card and reissue a new card when you report a problem. Unfortunately, these losses increase the cost of credit for all of us. **It is really important to review your credit card activity every month so that you**

can catch illegal activity on your card and report it promptly. If you've never experienced any credit card theft, then give it time. You will.

Debit cards can be very risky to use on-line since, unlike the credit cards that are backed by the banks that issue them, there is no one to replace your cash if the card is stolen.

When we pay bills directly from our bank account, then we need to provide the bank account information. You should only make payments directly from your bank account to other banks or reputable large companies (e.g., public utilities). Providing this information to smaller entities (that generally have fewer resources for information technology protection) exposes you to greater risk for having your information hacked.

There are many occasions when businesses and other organizations are asking you to provide your name, address, telephone number, or date-of-birth information. Why? It's because they want to add you to their mailing list. If maintaining contact with these folks is not important to you, then simply decline to provide the information. If they insist, then make something up for them. (Be creative. It can be fun!)

Here are some basic actions that you should take to reduce the chances for identity theft:

- Use complex passwords for sensitive accounts. Consider using a phrase or short sentence rather than a word or random-letter jumble. They're easier for you to remember.
- Don't re-use passwords for sensitive accounts.
- Don't carry your Social Security card with you. Only give out the number to reliable organizations and then, only when necessary.
- Don't leave your mail in a mailbox that others can access and steal from.
- Don't use debit cards for on-line purchases.
- Monitor your bank and credit card statements for unexpected activity every month.
- Shred all documents with personal information before putting them in the trash.
- Install anti-virus software on your computer.

- Erase the memory of your computer, phone or mobile device before you discard it or give it away.
- Do an annual check of your credit reports (i.e., Equifax, Experian, TransUnion, etc.). Consider freezing your reports if you're not planning to seek any new loans, mortgages or credit cards. This will prevent a thief from using your information to get credit approval in your name.

Finally, it's important to remember that all organizations can (and will) be hacked. Even the federal government and major banking institutions are not immune. Limiting the number of places where your private information is exposed is the best practice.

While it is true that banks take many precautions to protect themselves from hackers, even their computer systems are not completely foolproof. I had an interesting experience a few years ago when I went on-line to check the balance in my individual retirement account (IRA). The balance listed was approximately $1.3 billion. This was about $1.2999 billion more than the last time I checked the balance. You have no idea how exhilarating it was to see all of those zeros!

I immediately called my banker and thanked him for doing such a great job with the investments. I told him that I'd like to leave $300 million in the IRA and pick up a check for $1 billion the next day. After a long pause, he told me that he'd look into it. To my dismay, the less-exhilarating balance was restored in a few minutes after I hung up the phone. I was disappointed that I couldn't at least have been a billionaire-for-a-day. Plus, I really wanted to see how they could write all of those zeros on the check.

Recognize the True Costs of Our Activities

When we turn our attention to the earth's environment, we are just beginning to wake-up to the fact that dumping carbon dioxide (i.e., CO_2) waste into the atmosphere for several hundred years has a cost associated with it, and nobody has been paying the bill. We are creating big trouble for future generations. Fixing climate-change-related problems is going to be REALLY expensive, if we can fix it at all.

Our failure has been that we did not (and still do not) consider the actual life-cycle cost of our activities. The real cost of a ton of coal or a barrel of oil is not the cost to get it out of the ground, clean it up, ship it to a customer and charge a profit. The real cost is all of those things, PLUS the cost of disposing of the waste associated with the production AND USE of those fuels. But it's inconvenient to worry about cleaning up after the party, and besides, there's no one who has even cared about cleaning up until recently. Who wants to pay the full life-cycle cost of fossil fuels when you can get away with only paying for the front half?

The same story plays out when it comes to plastic waste. It's cheap to produce and expensive to recycle. Who wants to talk about the expense of recycling if all you have to do is to bury it in a landfill? Sure, some of the stuff gets out into our water supplies, and sure, it gives marine life a hard time, but who wants to pay for the full, life-cycle cost of plastic usage when nobody is forcing you to pay to recycle the stuff?

Plastic (and many other) manufacturers should be barred from producing unless they're willing to accept the return of their used products. If that was the case, then they'd be forced to add the cost of recycling into the selling price of the product. All of a sudden, we'd witness the immediate disappearance of Styrofoam peanuts from shipping containers. More sustainable and less-costly-to-recycle alternatives would quickly appear in their place.

There are "free-lunch" problems like these, all around us. It is ultimately unfair not to pay the full costs associated with our activities. Otherwise, we'll be leaving an unpaid debt to future generations. You and your children (if any) will struggle to deal with the problems that previous generations have failed to confront.

We need to understand the limitations of the earth's ecosystem. The human race has been quick to exploit the resources of the planet to improve living conditions. This is OK, but when we come to realize that this exploitation is destroying our ecosystem, then we must do something about it.

Today we know that we have caused the earth's climate to change. The only way to reverse these changes is through the global political process. This sometimes appears to be a hopeless mess. Many people in the world deny that the problem exists. Others work hard to prevent changes that would impair their wealth. It is important to understand that our planet earth doesn't care about global politics, ignorance, or human greed. The physico-chemical systems that regulate climate will cause temperatures to rise and change the entire equilibrium of the atmosphere until the beautiful balance that we have come to know is re-established into something a lot less beautiful. The process of re-establishing equilibrium will cause climate changes that are damaging to the majority of mankind. In the absence of significant action, we are headed for thousands of years of hard times for humanity. We can avert the disaster but it will be expensive and will require our immediate unwavering support of initiatives to reduce climate change. This is a cause that we must all support.

Chapter 5.

SHARPEN YOUR PEOPLE SKILLS: ENJOY LIFE TO THE MAX

Unless you're planning to be a monk, a cloistered nun, a prisoner in solitary confinement, or in COVID quarantine, you will be interacting with a lot of different people every day of your life. This chapter provides Boomer Dad's list of important social skills for an aspiring, fun-loving person.

Speak Effectively

It is important for your long-term success to be able to speak to groups of people. Effective speakers carefully consider and simplify the message that they are trying to convey before they utter a word. When they do speak, they are deliberate, speaking slowly and clearly with enough power to be heard.

Effective and popular speakers do not speak with their backs to the audience. They face the audience. Many of us have difficulty making direct eye contact with the people in the audience, but focusing our eyes on various spots at the rear of the room works almost as well. Effective speakers understand that most people are "threes" and follow the presentation format revealed in Chapter 3:

1) tell 'em what you're going to tell 'em.

2) tell 'em

3) tell 'em what you just told 'em.

Avoid jargon unless the audience you're addressing is likely to understand and appreciate it. Keep your presentation both brief and focused while letting your passion for the subject matter be on display. Use a few carefully chosen illustrative figures and pictures when possible. Minimize words on presentation slides while making sure their font sizes are large enough to read from the back of the room. Nothing will make an audience hit the "snooze" button faster than a muddled presentation given by a speaker who can't be heard or understood with presentation slides that are disorganized or unreadable.

Effective public speaking is a skill that takes practice to develop but it is worth the time. It's a huge confidence builder to know that you can do a good job delivering important information to a group of people.

"Now, tell us more about your fear of speaking in front of an audience."

Learn to Write (not Just Text!)

Like speaking, writing is a critically important skill. It is a skill that is disappearing, being driven to oblivion by our collective infatuation with text messaging. Unfortunately, text messaging ignores proper spelling, grammar and just about everything else that written documents value. Sure, it's efficient, timely and good enough for routine communication, but great ideas will rarely emerge from a text message. In the professional world where clear articulation of complex ideas is essential, good writers are always in demand. Those who can write clearly and succinctly enjoy better jobs and career success than those who can't.

The best writing is brief and to the point. The best writers revise their drafts to eliminate unnecessary words and to select words that concisely convey complex ideas. They focus on paragraph structure: an opening sentence, supporting sentences, and a conclusion or transition to the next paragraph. The ability to write a strong paragraph is a key skill.

"Yes, a winky face is correct... But in ancient times, the semicolon was actually used to separate archaic written devices known as 'complete sentences.'"

CartoonStock.com

Keep your sentences as simple as possible with clear subject/verb/object structure. Avoid run-on sentences. Modern word processors often provide spelling and grammar-checking functions. Use care when accepting these computerized suggestions; they're not always correct.

The goal is not to rival Shakespeare or Hemingway, but rather to simply communicate information as clearly as possible to others. With practice, your own style will emerge.

Today, most of us spend the majority of our writing time on email and/or texting. Using email and texts seems simple enough, but there are important differences between a quickly drafted email or text and letters to be sent via postal mail that are worth remembering:

- Email is most appropriate for brief communication related to a particular subject. The specific subject of the email should be included in the subject line. Longer narratives should be included as attachments rather than in the body of the email.
- Email and texts enable immediate communication. So if you are angry, inebriated, or upset, then you should consciously refrain from sending any messages until you've had a chance to return to your normal self and have regained a clear enough head to reflect on the message that you are going to send. Consciously refrain from sending repeated messages when you are not in a good frame of mind.
- Care is required to make sure that email and text messages are clear and won't be misconstrued. If you're not sure about whether or not you should say something in an email or text, then you probably shouldn't say it. A phone call or face-to-face conversation might be better.
- The "REPLY ALL" button is dangerous. Don't use it unless it is important for everyone on the thread to receive the information, otherwise you are just spamming people. If the information in the email is critical of others or controversial, then big problems can arise if it is sent to the wrong people.
- Avoid using all capital letters. This is regarded as SCREAMING AT SOMEONE.

- Email never goes away. It is stored on servers and on the computers of the recipients. Once you've hit the "SEND" button then you've lost control of the information in that message. Don't use email to send information that is very sensitive.

Balance All of It

Many of the struggles that we experience in life come from being caught in the middle of conflicting demands. We have personal ambitions, a career, a job, parents, siblings, friends, a spouse, children, hobbies, community commitments, etc., etc. The list goes on, and everyone in your world has different expectations of you. But sometimes a crisis on the job requires overtime just when you and your significant other were planning to celebrate an anniversary. Sometimes you have a sick child who needs to go to the doctor and you've got an important meeting scheduled at the same time. Common conflicts like these can drive you to despair.

All of us can only juggle so many things before everything comes crashing down. If only we could find more "balance" in our lives!!

Finding "balance" is hard because "balance" is an abstraction that only exists in our minds. There is no tangible "life-balance.". What we have is a personal pre-conceived idea of how we'd like our day to go, and when things don't go according to that plan, we get stressed and feel that our life is "out of balance."

When we are seeking more "balance" in our lives, we're really talking about seeking to better manage our stress. We have no control over the unexpected needs of our job, a sudden illness of a child, or a broken water pipe, and all contribute varying amounts of stress to our life. **In the moment of stress, all we can do is prioritize the emergencies and take appropriate action.** In medical emergencies this is called "triage."

Triage is a process of dividing victims of a disaster into three groups: a group of those who will be OK without immediate care; a group who will die without immediate care; and a group who will die even with care. This allows precious medical resources to be applied to those victims where it will make the biggest difference. Triage brings critical focus to handling a crisis.

With our personal emergencies, using triage is a good strategy. Some things are not going to be "fixed" by our immediate attention, and some things simply don't deserve our immediate attention. Just like in the world of medicine, **handle the emergency where your effort will have the biggest impact.**

When we use triage, we are acknowledging our limitations. We are accepting the fact that we can't fix everything all of the time, but we also can take comfort in the fact that we did the best that we could under the circumstances. This relieves our stress.

There are things that we can do to prepare for life's inevitable hiccups. We can try to do some advance planning and negotiating with our critical team members, especially our immediate team (i.e., spouse and our boss). So have a preemptive discussion about the likelihood of these unexpected emergencies.

Wherever you work, ask about what the acceptable options are for handling personal emergencies during working hours. Is it OK to handle

"O.K., now—on three, I'm going to toss a second job in there!"

the emergency and make up the time later? Does the boss need to be notified? Knowing what is acceptable to your boss can greatly reduce the stress of handling these situations. If your boss shows little flexibility in this area and seems to believe that the company's interests are superior to the needs of your family, then you'd be wise to begin looking for another job at an organization that cares more about its workers.

Having a similar discussion with your spouse is also important. Your spouse may have certain constraints that limit their flexibility to assist in handling an emergency. Knowing about these constraints in advance can help avoid stress for both of you.

Triage can be a very useful strategy for reducing our stress, but finding true "balance" sometimes requires a careful re-evaluation of how we define success in our lives. Lowering our expectations and cutting back on commitments is often a good starting point. Focusing less on status and prestige, and focusing more on the quality of your relationships and your physical well-being, can greatly improve the harmony in your life. Just say "no" to over-commitment. Focus on the moment and enjoy it when you can. Be mellow. Go with the flow. Enjoy the balance!

Learn to Cook

Is there anything more important? Fortunately, we usually eat three meals a day, so that's three opportunities to use and develop the skill every day! In a year, that's over a thousand practice opportunities. (In a lifetime, it could be 100,000 if you live to be 100.)

And there's more! Cooking is a craft that requires a team:

Hunter/gatherers to get the stuff that needs cooking.
Assistants to prepare the food for the cook to cook.
A cook (to cook).
Someone to eat what the cook has cooked.
Someone to clean up the mess that the cook and eaters have made.

Wow! What a great opportunity to socialize with the team, three times every day!

I must confess here that I can't cook. Furthermore, I'm getting close enough to the 100-year mark that I'm not likely to learn that skill. I have had the good fortune, for my entire life, of being surrounded by family who are excellent cooks. That's why I decided to specialize in the team-work of being the hunter/gatherer, eater, and cleanup guy. This decision was reinforced many years ago when one of my siblings told me that my cooking skills were "negligible."

In spite of this negative feedback, I decided that I needed to master a few meals so that I could feed myself (and others) reliably when the need arose. It's important for everyone to have a "go-to list" of meals that they can prepare. After years of reflection and countless forgettable experiences in the kitchen, I selected the following meals as my "signature" offerings:

Breakfast: Muffins, freshly baked from "Jiffy" Brand, Corn Muffin Mix with butter and honey (or jelly)
Lunch: Peanut butter and Jelly
Supper: Spaghetti (using sauce in a jar) with a side of microwaved peas
Dessert: Vanilla float (i.e., vanilla ice cream in cream soda)

So, if I'm doing the cooking, then that's what you're going to be eating. And of the items on the list, I have spent the most time exploring the peanut butter and jelly sandwich. To date, I have eaten at least 10,000 of these hand-held wonders. There is so much variety possible: crunchy peanut butter, smooth peanut butter, almond butter, cashew butter, sun-flower butter, grape jelly, grape jam, strawberry jelly, strawberry jam, cherry preserves, pear jam, raspberry jam, blueberry jam, honey, sliced banana, white bread, wheat bread, etc. This offers a lot of different com-binations of butters, breads and spreads. I never get bored (and you might not either). The single most important piece of advice that I can offer regarding peanut butter and jelly sandwiches is **go thick on the peanut butter**. Most recipes say use 2 tablespoons, but that's for weenies. Use 3 tablespoons, OR MORE! Screw the calories. Go big or go home!

I also recognize you, of course will have your own meal preferences. Scrambled eggs and toast perhaps? Ramen noodles? Cast-iron skillet cheeseburgers and baked beans? Whatever you choose to concoct, just make sure you clean up the mess (unless someone else on your team takes over that responsibility for the meal!).

"WE'RE OUT OF PEPPERS, SO I THREW IN A SCORPION TO SPICE UP OUR STEW."

CartoonStock.com

Figure Out the Diet That's Best for You

The most important thing to learn about eating is what diet is best for you. Your optimal diet would provide all the nourishment that you need along with the pleasure of being satisfied by the meal. Your optimal diet would do this while allowing you to maintain what you believe is a comfortable and healthy body weight. **Only you can figure out what you like to eat, what satisfies you and what allows you to maintain the body weight with which you're comfortable.**

The one observation that I can share is that most of us get accustomed to portion sizes that are too big. Somehow we "grow" to need that large portion in order to feel satisfied by the meal, and this begins a spiral to ever-increasing weight gain. One path to weight control is to decrease our portion sizes gradually over time.

"IT'S PARTLY GLANDULAR AND PARTLY 8,500 CALORIES PER DAY."

There's no magic here. It's **thermodynamics**. The First Law of Thermodynamics simply states that energy (in the form of "calories") is conserved. It cannot be created or destroyed. That means that the only way to maintain a constant body weight is to match the caloric energy that you are taking in by eating, with the caloric energy that your body is using for metabolism and exercise. But metabolic rates can vary considerably from person to person, making weight management a highly personal issue.

We can't do much about the calories that our bodies burn unless we commit ourselves to a really significant exercise regimen. (This takes a lot of willpower.) Unless we have such a regimen in place, the calories that we eat and don't burn get converted to fat. "Simply" reducing the calories that we eat is not easy because we immediately run into the problem of not feeling satisfied. Reducing food intake requires a lot of willpower to deal with our food cravings. **The bottom line is that weight control demands a lot of willpower no matter what path we choose.** Finding a way to manage our weight is important for our long-term health and happiness. Small steps today might make large steps unnecessary tomorrow.

But there's more to eating than just nourishment and satisfying our cravings. Eating is very often a social event where we interact with others. Any social activity invokes the necessity of minding our manners and following social norms for the activity.

When dining publicly it's important to be properly dressed for the venue and occasion, and to be punctual about arriving at the reservation time. Be cordial with the waiters and wait until everyone is seated and served before starting to eat. Put your napkin on your lap, don't chew with your mouth open, and don't speak with food in your mouth. It's all about showing **respect** for others.

Even when we're not in public and enjoying a casual dinner at home, there are customs that are worth considering. Dinnertime is a great opportunity for families to gather and share stories about the day's activities. It's also a good time to conduct family business and coordinate plans for the next day. Dinner should be a time when the focus is on the people seated at the table. Everyone should have a time to speak, and cellphones and TVs should be turned off. This is a way to show **respect** for those gathered and to welcome their conversation.

Be Well-Mannered

Having good manners is not an affectation of pompous rich folks. It all gets back to having a core value of respect for other people. Being well-mannered is an important way that we can show respect to others every day.

We respect people by saying please and thank you. We respect people by being punctual and well-groomed for appointments. We respect people by promptly responding to invitations and thanking people for gifts. We respect our family members when we clean up any mess that we make. We respect people when we offer to help them when they are struggling to carry something or to open a door.

Be sure to offer your seat to the person with a cane standing on the subway or the pregnant mother-to-be. Look out for elderly relatives and neighbors, and pleasantly offer your assistance when it seems needed. It all may seem pretentious and corny. It is not.

There are many good books on etiquette that make it easy to familiarize yourself with the currently accepted norms for good manners. You can't go wrong with "Emily Post's Etiquette, 19th edition. It's a classic reference with good advice. Another book that is worth the time is "Minding Miss Manners in an Era of Fake Etiquette" by Judith Martin. Miss Manner's obvious despair with the current state of etiquette provides some hilarious reading as she reviews some of the outrageous things that people do today. Her advice is always good and her trademark sweet words are occasionally dipped in a sarcastic sauce.

Don't Get Sucked into the Zombie Apocalypse

We are actually living in a real zombie apocalypse. The millions (maybe billions?) of zombies surrounding us haven't been infected by a weird virus from the bite of another zombie. They've been infected by an electronic smartphone worm that has burrowed into their brains and they're trapped in an alternative universe with other phone zombies that demands their continuous attention.

You see them walking down the street with a small rectangular screen held in front of their face, oblivious to their surroundings and bumping into people, cars, and obstacles. You see them in groups seated in restaurants, communicating with other zombies on their phone and not engaging with the people at the table with them (unless they're texting to each other rather than talking). You see them weaving around on the highway while they attempt to drive. (This is some bad sh*t!)

Zombies prioritize a text message that has just popped into their screen over the rare live conversation that they are having with a person standing in front of them. Is it possible to be any more rude? Even if they're not texting at the precise moment, this Boomer Dad believes it's likely they're playing some stupid online game, looking at some silly Tik-Tok or YouTube video, or posting their latest information on Facebook about the cool cellphone protector that they just found.

Get a grip! Live your life! Don't be sucked into this cesspool!

CartoonStock.com

If you are in the company of others and you receive an important call or text that requires your immediate response, be kind enough to excuse yourself from the group and conduct your business in a quiet location that doesn't interrupt the conversation of others.

Learn to Dance

I know people who have spent their lives trying to avoid social activities where dancing might occur. What a shame. Dancing is a blast. Unlike singing, you don't have to be good at it. You just need to be willing to try.

If it doesn't come naturally then don't be a wallflower; take some dancing lessons. It is valuable to at least know how to do a basic Foxtrot or Waltz since these are common at weddings.

There are many dance styles you can explore though. Modern hip-hop requires reasonably good physical conditioning if you're going to "bust-a-move" and not regret it. Tango can be very sensual and is fun to practice, especially with the right partner. Latin music is hard to listen to without feeling the need to dance. The Rhumba, Meringue and Cha-Cha are fun.

If you start appreciating dance, consider throwing dance parties with a particular dance theme. We once did a Bossa-Nova party with dance instructors on hand to help people get the moves right. It was fabulous.

Learn to Drink

"Everything in moderation" is the critical thought here. We all have different, biochemically based tolerances to alcohol. Some of us cannot drink without becoming deliriously drunk very quickly. Others can knockback considerably more without having their senses seriously degraded. Some of us should not drink at all (especially true if there is a family history of alcoholism. The susceptibility to alcohol addiction has a significant genetic basis.).

There's a lot to know about "how" to drink if you plan to do so. The first thing is to **know how much you can drink.** If you are planning to drive a car, then this is easy to estimate because most states have a blood alcohol limit of 0.08% blood alcohol concentration (BAC). The amount that you can drink depends primarily on gender (due to reduced alcohol dehydrogenase enzyme levels in women) and body weight. For example, if you are a 100-pound lady, then (1) drink will bring you to 0.07% BAC. If you are a 220-pound guy, then (3) drinks will probably take you to the 0.08% BAC limit. That's one way (i.e., the legal way) to think about alcohol limits.

When you will be travelling with a designated (i.e., non-drinking), driver then the situation is different. The question becomes how much can you actually drink before you "lose it? In this context, "lose it" has a broad meaning. It could be the point at which your speech is slurred, your balance is not great and/or your judgement is really impaired. It could also mean the point where you forcibly eject the alcohol (along with everything else that you've consumed) onto your friends nearby and the Persian rug that you're standing on.

Determining your personal "lose-it" point is not easy and requires a lot of experimentation. Most of us normally do this when we are teenagers, but is one of the most dangerous empirical studies that we can perform. **This experimentation is dangerous because our "lose-it" points are not a constant. They depend on our current physical condition, what we've eaten recently and the specifics of the type of drink that we are consuming.**

The details matter. It is especially important to recognize whether you are drinking normal sized portions of alcohol (i.e., 1 ounce or less of pure ethanol per drink). Beer is typically 6% alcohol (although some craft beers can be in the 3% to 9% range) and is served in 12 oz bottles, so each bottle contains about 0.7 ounces of pure ethanol. Wine is typically about 15% alcohol and a standard pour is 5 ounces, resulting in about 0.75 ounces of alcohol. Most cocktails can have 2 ounces of gin or vodka at about 80-proof (i.e., 40% alcohol), resulting in about 0.8 ounces of alcohol. If you're getting large pours, "doubles" or drinking draft beer out of a 32-oz Slurpee cup, then all bets are off. Once you start getting to 2 ounces or more of ethanol, then you're definitely getting into the danger zone. Anything more than (3) drinks and you can count on being impaired and probably a morning-after hangover.

What causes a hangover? Hangovers primarily result from dehydration caused by the diuretic effect of alcohol—and the fact that you probably haven't been drinking any water while drinking the alcohol. Hangovers are enhanced by the presence of congeners (i.e., fermentation products like methanol, furfural, tannins, etc., found in the alcohol) and high levels of acetaldehyde produced by the normal enzymatic conversion of ethanol. Many people have more hangover trouble if they mix different types of alcohol (e.g., a beer followed by a cocktail followed by a glass of wine). Some people find that taking an antacid and drinking water before consuming alcoholic beverages to be helpful at reducing hangover severity.

Finally, there are two things that you must do whenever you've consumed alcohol. First, drink water to rehydrate your body. As a rule of thumb, drink one glass of water for each drink that you've had. Second, if you've got alcohol in your body, DO NOT TAKE TYLENOL or any medication containing acetaminophen since the risk of liver damage is very high. Use ibuprofen instead.

Learn to Plan

Life is short. It makes sense to try to get the most from the time that we have on this planet. **Planning is the key to achieving that goal.**

Planning involves careful consideration of what resources and actions will be necessary to reach the goal. We all develop plans when we think about the meals that we'd like to eat and prepare a list of things that we'll need to buy at the grocery store to make those meals possible. Some of us are good planners and so we get everything that we need in one trip to the store. Poor planners waste a lot of time (and fuel!) making multiple trips that could have been avoided by exerting a few more minutes of careful thought before the first trip. Planning can make our lives easier and less stressful.

More elaborate goals require more careful planning. Historically, virtually all major accomplishments such as the Apollo moon landings, the first expedition to reach the south pole, or the summit of Mount Everest, etc., can trace their success to the extensive planning that went into the mission. Expeditions that failed can often trace their failure to inadequate planning. Excellent planning was the "secret-weapon" that brought victory to General Dwight Eisenhower's D-Day invasion, a turning point in World War II.

Careful planning requires a focused imagination along with accurate knowledge of the mission elements and risks: What sequence of events is needed to reach the goal? What can go wrong with each event? How likely is this to happen? How bad would it be if it *did* happen? What can be done to mitigate each risk?

It is not unusual to abandon a proposed mission after asking those questions. A little bit of careful thought before beginning a project or activity can keep us out of trouble.

Here are some Four Key Steps to a Smart Plan that are worth considering:

1) Clearly define the specific goal that you want to achieve.
2) Work backward from the goal to define the major steps needed to reach the goal.
3) If possible, break the steps into smaller chunks with associated checkpoints that allow you to measure your progress.
4) Identify those steps that require significant resources and decide whether those resources are available. If not, then consider revising the plan.

Once you have a good plan and start heading toward your goal, then don't be surprised if everything doesn't go according to the plan. Plans are "living" documents that usually need to be revised to accommodate unanticipated events.

Revising a plan is not an indication of failure, and it is often jokingly said that plans are the best descriptions of what will probably *not* happen. Nevertheless, plans are very useful because the provide a guide for making the important decisions that will lead us to the goal that we're seeking. It is an old adage (often erroneously attributed to Ben Franklin) that, "If you fail to plan, you are planning to fail." People who have a carefully considered plan and the desire to execute it are always a formidable force.

Learn to Listen

Good listeners tend to be very popular, but the reality is most of us are not good listeners. Those people who actually listen to other people are rare. Fortunately listening is a social skill that we can develop.

Many of us dread the prospect of making small talk in social situations where there are a lot of new people. You can reduce the anxiety you feel if you consciously place yourself in "listening mode.". Do so by preparing (in advance) a few generic ice-breaker questions that you can ask the person standing next to you. First introduce yourself, then use one of these (or create some better ones!):

- What's your favorite place of all the places you've travelled?
- If you could go to Mars, would you? Why or why not?
- If money was not a concern, what job would you choose?
- What is the last TV show that you binge-watched?
- What do you really think about wave/particle duality?

People are usually comfortable talking about themselves, so relax and just listen to them. They'll enjoy your interest in them, and you don't have to say much beyond asking them a few more follow-up questions. They might then reciprocate and ask a question about you. *Presto!* You're having a conversation.

Beyond its value for making small talk, listening is the ability to accurately receive the message that another person is trying to communicate. This is a skill that takes a lot of work. It goes beyond the simple strategy of being attentive and not talking while someone else is speaking. Many times, a speaker cannot easily articulate what they are trying to communicate. A good listener will create a relaxed atmosphere for the conversation and ask questions to try to clarify the point of what the speaker is saying. Good listeners pay attention to non-verbal cues (e.g., "body-language") to interpret what is being said. One mistake that I often make when "listening" is jumping in and trying to offer solutions to a problem that is being revealed by the speaker. This is an attempt to be helpful, but it is not listening.

Truly listening to others can help them solve problems, whether at work or in their personal life. For example, I have spent a great deal of time working on teams of scientists and engineers. In the course of trying

A. BACALL

"It's nothing to worry about nurse. It's only teeth bites on your tongue. Lots of good listeners have them."

to understand some weird experimental results or solve a thorny technical problem, it is very common for people to get to points where they don't know how to proceed. I have found that the best way to clear the logjam is to take a break, sit down in a quiet spot and ask the person to talk me through the problem. In most cases the problem gets resolved, not because I could offer anything constructive, but rather because it allowed the speaker to organize their thoughts and present them systematically, thereby allowing them to recognize potential holes or errors in their methodology. **Listening thus is a powerful management tool.**

When people are dealing (struggling) with personal issues, listening can really help friends or family members who may be going through a crisis. It is often the case that we can't do much to help them except by being a good listener as they try to work through their predicament. **Listening is a gift that anyone can offer at any time, and it is always an appropriate thing to do.**

Go to the Funeral

Nobody likes going to funerals. Nobody. Funerals are usually sad.

Get over it. It's not about you. It's about your friend, acquaintance or family member who is no longer drinking, eating and dancing with you. It is your duty to show up and pay your respect. The grieving family is always grateful to know that their loved one is missed by others. When it's your time to go, you'd be grateful for those who showed up in your honor and supported those whom you loved in your time here on earth.

Understand Politics

Politics define the process of making the laws that we must abide as citizens. It necessarily involves messy debates, conflicts, differences of opinion and compromises. So as German statesman and diplomat Otto von

Bismarck keenly observed, "Laws are like sausages, it is better not to see them being made."

As distasteful as politics may be at times, it is an activity that requires the participation of all responsible citizens. This has been recognized since the time of ancient Greece when Plato pointed out, "One of the penalties for refusing to participate in politics is that you end up being governed by your inferiors."

What are your political leanings? Surely, they are oriented by your core values (Chapter 1). And I have come to believe that it doesn't matter so much whether you are a "conservative" or a "liberal". **What matters is your willingness to respect the positions of your political adversaries and to listen to their reasoning in an attempt to find "common ground."**

One thing that has become clear in the hyper-polarized political world of today is that both the Democratic Party and Republican Party are the same in their delusional thinking. They both think that their way is the only way. Essentially, take it or leave it.

"He tells it like it is."

CartoonStock.com

This approach doesn't work. Ideologues can't really do politics. They can only cram things down the throat of the minority. True politics are pragmatic. Unfortunately, as of this writing, honest and pragmatic politicians are not as abundant as we'd like. **Effective politics involve listening and compromise.**

Accordingly, moderates are the only people who can do the "heavy lifting" of politics. They are the "listeners" (see previous section in this chapter on how important this social skill is!) willing to strike a fair deal.

Be a moderate conservative or a moderate liberal. Stick to your core values. Recognize that your political adversaries are your neighbors and that you both share the same great country. You are fellow Americans, not enemies.

Political debates are full of rhetorical fallacies that obstruct the open exchange of ideas. The politicians present deliberately distort the facts and attempt to distract any audience with emotional appeals. The resulting fallacies are the enemy of sound reasoning. Be aware of these deceits and don't be suckered by them.

Here's a short list of some of the more common rhetorical fallacies that we see every day:

1. **Misdirection.** *Attempts to distract the audience from the real issue to focus instead on something else that the speaker wants to talk about.*

   Example: "I understand that you want to know what happened at the Senate Judiciary committee. What is really important is to talk about whether the federal government is going to help our veterans."

2. **Absurd Extrapolation.** *Tries to convince the audience that a policy that takes a small step in one direction will lead to an avalanche of events that will cause drastic change.*

   Example: If we start requiring background checks for gun purchases, then the government will know who has the guns and will confiscate them.

3. **Strawman Fallacy.** *Intentionally misrepresents an opponent's position to set up an easy (but false) target for the speaker to destroy.*

   Example: "Senator Jones says the nation should not increase the defense budget. Senator Smith says that he cannot believe that Senator Jones is willing to leave the nation defenseless."

4. **Circular Reasoning.** *Here, the speaker begins with what they are trying to end with, thereby providing no evidence to support the conclusion.*

   Example: "The news is fake because so much of the news is fake."
   Example: "You must obey the law because it's illegal to break the law."

5. **Post-Hoc ("false cause") Fallacy.** *Confuses correlation with causation.*

   Example: "A Democratic president was elected, and then I had a car wreck. The Democratic president caused my car wreck."

6. **False Dilemma.** *Presents only two options when there are many options.*

   Example: "America: love it or leave it".

Now you're prepared to recognize and ignore these types of bogus arguments when you're bombarded with political rhetoric.

Dealing with Conflict

Most people do not like conflict. We all want to be liked, and so it is normal for many of us to side-step a conflict, even when avoiding it causes negative consequences.

We often do this with co-workers who are not pulling their weight or behaving badly. If it's not too bad, then we simply put up with it and try to ignore it. The same can happen with roommates, spouses, friends and family members. Walking away and ignoring the problem is reasonable when the conflicts are minor and occurring infrequently. What do you do when the conflict is more severe and/or frequent? Is conflict avoidance still a good strategy?

Generally, conflict avoidance is a bad strategy. It allows bad behavior to persist and causes stress. Fundamentally, it is dishonest to pretend that everything is fine when it is not. What should you do? Here's a **5-Step Plan for Handling Conflict:**

Step 1:   Cool off. Carefully review the conflict situation. Are you doing anything to cause or aggravate the conflict? What specifically is the other party doing that you find offensive? Now put yourself in their shoes. Are they within their rights to behave as they do? After an honest assessment, it is not unusual to come to a realization that you share equal blame for the conflict.

Step 2:   If you don't believe that you owe the other party an apology, then clearly define the main item that you find to be offensive. Work on being able to communicate this item clearly.

Step 3:   Arrange to talk about it with the other party in the conflict. Calmly approach the other party and ask them if you might start a discussion. Use a non-threatening and respectful approach along these lines: "I've got a problem that I need to tell you about. Is this a convenient time for you?"

Step 4:   Calmly describe the problem. **Say what you mean, but don't say it mean!** Listen to what the other person has to say. Ask questions to see how the conflict might be resolved. Understand that win-win solutions are the most durable.

Step 5:   If the other party agrees to help resolve the problem, then offer a handshake, a hug, or a kind word.

Congratulations, you've made progress. If not, then spit in their coffee cup and get ready for war. *Game on!*

It is also useful to consider those rare instances when unprovoked conflict arises very suddenly (as in a mugging). You're walking along, minding your own business, and a thug decides to threaten you. Turn and run if you can. But what if you can't run away? What do you do?

Professional fighters will tell you that the best thing that you can do is to **try to de-escalate the situation.** Immediately take a step backwards and raise your hands in a surrender gesture. (This moves you away from the assailant and places your arms in a good position to block any punches thrown.) Look them in the eye and tell the mugger that you don't want any trouble. Ask what they want. If they want your money, then throw them your wallet. **Don't argue with them… just keep moving away from them!**

If that doesn't end the confrontation and you think that you're going to be attacked, then your focus should be on controlling any weapon that they might have. If you have an opening to defend yourself, then the two best moves are a hard kick to the groin, followed by a hard punch to the chin or nose. Never punch with a closed fist because you will hurt your hand. Use the heel of your open hand. Yell for help and try to escape. For better preparation, consider taking a self-defense class.

I've been fortunate to have avoided these types of dangerous confrontations. I credit good situational awareness for steering me clear. Physical violence is never a good option, but sometimes it happens because it's necessary. I will confess that as a small fourth grader, punching the big class bully in the nose was not only satisfying but effective. He never bothered me again.

Parenting

Perhaps the most profound and complex duty we have as human beings is raising the little people who are born into our families. Few young parents are ever truly prepared for the job, but all will find their way. Besides providing for the food, clothing and shelter needs of children, parents are the most important teachers and protectors. Parents teach by their words and their deeds. Little kids don't miss anything. They hear every word. They sense every mood. They witness every act of kindness. They witness every act of cruelty. The core values of most kids are formed by observing their parent's behavior long before they go to school.

Kids need **boundaries** as they grow, and these boundaries need to move as they mature. Boundaries simplify the world with which kids need to deal. Boundaries protect them until they are ready to advance to a new set. Parents are the ones responsible for setting the boundaries. Set the boundaries too narrow and the child gets frustrated and can't explore the new things that interest them. Set them too wide and the child can encounter things they're not equipped to handle. So being attentive to the child's development and moving the boundaries appropriately is a key job of the parents.

Allowing kids to fail is a part of this process. We learn at least as much from our failures as we do from our good experiences. Good parenting is about allowing our kids to explore the limits of their abilities but being there to serve as their safety net when they fall off the cliff.

Another critical skill that parents need to develop is **consistency**. Both parents need to be on the same page as far as rules and boundaries are concerned. If not, the kids will figure this out and game the more lenient parent whenever possible. If children are told that they can't do something, then both parents need to stick with that rule until it's time to change that boundary. If the boundary a parent gives to their kid differs from that of the other parent, then effectively there are no established boundaries. Both parents will lose control of their child until new, mutually-agreed-upon boundaries are established.

Staying engaged with the kids as they mature requires a light touch. They want to be independent. You want to know what they're up to, and if they're doing OK. They probably can't clearly articulate the things that bother them (and they don't want to tell you anyway). The key is **listening and observing.**

My sister shared with me her strategy for keeping up with her kids. She insisted on being the "taxi service." She'd take her kids and their friends who were going to an activity, whether sports, dance, or something else, and listen while they chattered away in the back seat. Once she did a little bit of information-sharing with the other parents, the parents were able to connect many dots about what was going on in their kids' lives.

As kids do get great satisfaction from doing things themselves and accomplishing goals independently, parents need to stand back and let them try to do things their way. Many times, they will fail, but failure can be the best teacher. Parents help by staying in the background but being one step ahead of the kids and making a rescue plan to save them from a catastrophic crash-and-burn. Our children are going to fall off their bikes. They are going to scrape their knees. Just make sure they're not doing so in heavy traffic. The overall aim is to help them build self-confidence without being seriously injured.

Eventually, some of us are lucky enough to be blessed with grandchildren. The experience of grandparenting is very different from that of parenting. It is greatly simplified because the regular conflicts that often get in the way of parent-child relationships are rarer in grandparent-grandchild relationships.

The greatest gift that a grandparent can bestow on a grandchild is **attention**. Spend individual time with them. Listen to what they have to say. Play games with them. Ask them to help you work in the garden or cook a meal. They'll love you for it, and you will experience enormous joy when you see them discover new things.

Being a Friend

Ralph Waldo Emerson said, "The only way to have a friend is to be one." Finding a friend is a delicate process, worthy of great care. Friendships happen when we accept the other person for whom they are, accepting their faults as well as their virtues. True friends don't put you down. They show you respect, listen to you and make you laugh. They also laugh at your jokes (!), are fun to be around, and are dependable. Friendships require some effort to maintain, especially when friends live in distant locations. Friendships require nurturing. The time invested for communicating and getting together is a small price for such a valuable gift.

The process of making friends was explored almost 100 years ago by Dale Carnegie in his famous self-help book, "How to Win Friends and Influence People." He presented some simple ideas that are still fresh today:

- Don't criticize others or complain.
- Be forgiving.
- Offer praise and sincere appreciation.
- Smile.
- Be a good listener.
- Make the other person feel important. Inquire about their interests.
- Let the other person do the talking.
- Show respect for other people's opinions.
- If you're wrong, then admit it promptly.
- Ask a question rather than give an order.
- Give the other person a fine reputation to live up to.

It's a lot more fun to make friends rather than enemies. Besides, Thomas Jones (a math teacher at Cambridge University) once made a very accurate observation: "Friends may come and go but enemies accumulate." This is an important fact to recognize and remember.

Being a Good Partner

Many of us are fortunate enough, at some point, to find a partner to share life's joys and sorrows. It is wonderful to have another person whom you can trust and rely upon for support.

Being a good partner is a two-way street, however. If you expect your partner to be trustworthy and reliable, then you too must be trustworthy and reliable. A key ingredient of successful partnerships is **complete acceptance of your partner for who they are, strengths and weaknesses included.**

CartoonStock.com

We all seek balance and harmony in our partnerships. Balance and harmony are often achieved, but not always. Enduring the imbalances and reconciling them can be painful, difficult and damaging to the partnership.

Why do imbalances occur? There are probably as many reasons as there are partnerships. Perhaps the main source of imbalance comes from our pre-conceived expectations of how the partnership will actually work, and such notions often come from the families in which we grew up. They come from societal norms too, as well as from individual fears and aspirations.

There are significant gender influences causing the imbalance. Specifically, in patriarchal Western cultures it was customary for the husband in the family to be the breadwinner and head of the household. Likewise, it was customary for the wife to be responsible for the children and housekeeping. If such role-models meet the expectations of the partners, then marital harmony is within reach. However, while this arrangement worked for a long time, it has become a quaint anachronism in modern Western societies.

Think about this: Which job actually requires more work? A hundred or more years ago, great physical strength was required to be a lumberjack, coal miner or bricklayer, so men gravitated to those jobs. Women were left with the strenuous work of housekeeping in a home without washing machines or other appliances. Organized activities for kids back then were very limited, making child-rearing and housekeeping very strenuous but less complicated than it is today. It could be (weakly) argued that these partnership roles had reasonable balance in the daily rituals that were common a hundred years ago. The situation today is totally different: Very few jobs demand great physical strength, making them accessible to men and women alike. As we have become increasingly affluent, with many labor-saving appliances, housekeeping is (perhaps) less strenuous but much more complex. The logistics of raising a family have become extremely challenging with the expectations that the children will all be well-groomed, transported to school in a timely manner, and enrolled in a suitable array of extracurricular activities from pre-school to high school.

The logistical complexity of keeping the family operation running manifests itself in the form of "emotional labor." (and sometimes physical, depending on whether there is a physical tantrum in play). This is the relentless effort required to juggle all of the routine, obligatory tasks (e.g., preparing breakfast, getting the kids dressed, combing the children's hair, etc.) along with those "exceptional" events (e.g., taking the kids for a dentist appointment while dropping off the dog at the kennel, etc.). Emotional labor is often overlooked in many partnerships and leads to imbalance and unhappiness.

In today's entrepreneurial and "gig" economies, jobs have become more logistically complex as well, requiring great flexibility in scheduling work and tolerating work hours outside of the normal hours of 9 to 5. This adds "emotional labor" to the breadwinners in a partnership.

The balance of labor in many partnerships today has really shifted. Arguably (and probably, in my opinion) the workload of the stay-at-home homemaker partner arguably now exceeds that of the "breadwinning" partner, especially if one considers the emotional labor involved. And if both partners are working breadwinners, then it becomes totally unfair for one partner to shoulder the burden of working, childrearing and housekeeping. So this is a major source of stress and imbalance in many households today.

Many partners (notably men) never take responsibility for many of the child-rearing and home-making chores, and while they are aware of the physical labor required for these tasks, they are simply unaware of the very significant emotional labor required. I am guilty of being one of those people: My partner was a working breadwinner who successfully managed the logistics of child-rearing. As our children grew, I failed to fully appreciate the magnitude of this effort when it was happening. I am in my partner's debt for those years of unbalanced emotional labor.

The key to reconciling imbalances is for each partner to open their mind to discussing the situation, identifying the perceived inequities and committing to a fair rearrangement of responsibilities. This is usually hard to do, as each partner often sees the inequities differently. It can take a lot of discussion before each partner comes to an adequate understanding of the other's pain. Some partners are resistant to any form of compromise, and without compromise, there will be no reconciliation.

Ultimately, **any fair solution requires that the partner with fewest responsibilities assume some responsibilities from the partner with the most.** In my parenting life it wasn't practical for me to take over responsibilities for buying clothes or fixing the hair for my three daughters (since this Boomer Dad already had a reputation as a long-time fugitive from the style-police). What was practical for me to assume most of the chauffeuring and routine shopping activities. Perfect balance was not achieved with this compromise, but the partnership was preserved... and it continues happily to this day.

Throw a Great Party

Parties are fun but great parties are unforgettable. Great parties don't just happen, they're carefully planned (usually by my brilliant spouse). Here are the key elements to consider:

a) Theme: Picking a good theme is the single most important factor. Choose a theme that is exotic, intriguing, or unconventional. That theme will determine:
- the best time of year to have the party,
- the best location for the party,
- the best people to invite who will enjoy that theme
- the decorations
- the style of costumes (if desired)

b) Guest List   Prepare a list of those whom you'd like to invite. With your chosen theme in mind, consider inviting new faces who are not part of the usual group and might really enjoy the theme. For example, if it's a dance party, then invite people who can dance. Invite both the young and the old for diversity and interest. The size of your guest list will determine the size of an appropriate venue and the amount of food and drink required. Keep in mind that not everyone invited will be able to come, so if you want to have 50 people show up, consider inviting 60.

c) Venue   If the party will be held someplace other than your home, then reserve a venue large enough to accommodate the expected attendance. Do this early in the planning process as it's not unusual for popular venues to be booked months in advance. Even if you're having the event at your home, there may be things that you need to rent (e.g., a tent, tables, chairs, etc.). Book those that are needed as early as possible to avoid a last-minute crisis. If you're planning an outdoor event, then be sure to have a backup plan if the weather fails to cooperate.

d) Invitations   An artistically crafted invitation will show the invited guests that this event is being well planned and worth their time. The aim is to create excitement and anticipation for the party. It will communicate the theme clearly and provide all of the necessary guidance, which should include:
- Date, time, location
- Parking instructions
- Food/beverage plans
- Dress code, costume suggestions, etc.

It is very important to get invitations out to the guest list at least a month before the event. (Two months would be better.) People have busy schedules. With that in mind, it's prudent to select a date and time that is unlikely to conflict with other activities.

d) Music   Depending on the party's theme, live music may not be necessary, but great parties usually have wild dancing (and that takes good music). If you're planning to have a band or DJ, then, like with the venue, these folks need to be booked well in advance. There are great bands and great DJs, and generally, you get what you pay for. Yet whether it's a band or a DJ that will be providing the music, they need to be managed (by you, I mean). Based on the theme, select the genres of music that you want to hear. Select a band or DJ that can deliver that genre. Meet with them in advance to review their playlist and performance schedule proposal. Coordinate their performance schedule with other events that might be planned for the party so that the band isn't playing a waltz when the stripper busts out of the cake. Talk to the band or DJ about sound levels too. Most bands and DJs have equipment that is designed to fill a stadium with sound, and they are just too loud for smaller venues. Loud music prevents the guests from having any conversation, and guests are not coming to the party to hear the DJ or band; they're coming to hang out with friends. Many bands and DJs don't get that, but good bands and DJs will understand. FYI, they are likely to require a contract before they'll accept the gig, so be sure that your preferred music and sound levels are addressed in the contract.

e) Decorations   The venue should be decorated to support the theme of the party. Engage friends who have an artistic flair to participate in the choice (or creation) of decorations, with you paying for any necessary supplies, of course. (Guys, if you're having the party in your garage then you may need a lot of decoration.)

f) Food   Great parties have great food. Once again, consider the theme, arranging for some unusual food items that are consistent with the theme. Also be sure to have some vegan food options if you're inviting those kinds of weirdos to the party. Having food will allow guests to arrive earlier and stay longer. More fun!

g) Drinks   Plan to offer a spectrum of non-alcoholic (e.g., bottled water, soft drinks, juices) and alcoholic beverages (e.g., beer, wine, whiskeys). If the party is large enough, consider hiring a bartender for the evening. Encourage guests to have a designated driver or an Uber reservation if they're planning to do some serious partying.

h) Surprise   Include an unexpected surprise at the event. If it's Christmas, then invite Santa Claus. At Halloween have a fortune teller drop in, or a group of guests who are willing to do a witches' dance around a bon-fire. If it's a dance party, then have a dance instructor available. The surprise could also be a gift bag with some theme-appropriate trinkets. Or you might arrange for some guys dressed as policemen to raid the party and handcuff everybody. Use your imagination.

Big parties are great, but it is important to celebrate less significant events too. Celebration brings people together for the purpose of giving thanks and rejoicing over notable achievements. It pulls us into the moment. What could be better? We should do it whenever the slightest opportunity presents itself.

Be the person who is always ready to raise a glass to toast the achievements of others. Informal celebrations here are often the best since they don't require elaborate preparation and you can do it more frequently. Be the prepared person by keeping suitable snacks and libations on hand so that a celebration can commence the moment that a few people arrive. Celebration makes life worth living. Do it whenever possible.

Chapter 6.

You Don't Have to Be a Boy (or Girl) Scout to Be Prepared

We devote a lot of our life to preparing for it. For most of us, the first 18 years are spent going to school, playing sports, learning etiquette, earning a driver's license and generally preparing us to assume responsibility for our adult lives. But there's much more to preparedness than classroom learning.

We're talking about preparing ourselves physically, mentally, financially and materially to face life's challenges. It's about developing personality traits that make us strong and resilient; learning to recognize the sometimes weird behavior of those around us; and developing social skills that will give us the tools to navigate that weirdness and enjoy life to the fullest. It is also about learning to accurately assess the risks that we might face so that we can take appropriate steps to reduce those risks.

Risk Assessment

When engineers are designing a new product, they often spend a lot of time doing "Design Failure Modes and Effects Analysis" (DFMEA). Stay with me here, because this important work is focused on scrutinizing every element of the product for ways that it can fail, along with the probability and severity of those potential failures.

An arbitrary scale is used to rate the probability of a particular failure (e.g., 0 = impossible, 10 = guaranteed to happen). A similar scale is used to rate the severity of the failure (e.g., 0 = nobody would even notice, 10 = we're all dead). Each failure mode is rated for its likely probability and severity, with the two ratings multiplied to provide a quantitative risk factor (e.g., 0 = no risk, 100 = maximum risk). An acceptable risk threshold value is established, and the risk associated with each design element is compared to that acceptable value. If the risk is greater than the acceptable threshold, then some change needs to be made to the design to bring the risk for that element below the acceptable threshold. This quantitative approach allows expensive engineering resources to be devoted to fixing those risks that matter and ignoring those risks that don't.

Almost no one does a detailed quantitative risk analysis of daily activities that we are about to initiate. Most of us don't even spend much time thinking about what can go wrong, and even if we do, then fewer still have an accurate idea of the probability of that occurrence. **Yet a few minutes of thought and preparation for an afternoon outing can make the difference between a wonderful excursion… and the trip from hell.**

Baloo

"Oh, come on — You only live once!"

CartoonStock.com

If we accept the notion that the path of our lives is determined by the decisions that we make, then **having an accurate understanding of the relative risks associated with our choices is really important.** Many people make bad decisions because they lack an understanding of the risks that they are taking with their decision.

As an example, when you go to the beach, you face a number of well-known risks. Most people would say that their greatest fears are of sharks and drowning. What about you… Have you thought about the risks of going to the beach and swimming? Have you done anything to reduce those risks? Do you know what the biggest risk might be?

The National Oceanographic and Atmospheric Agency (NOAA) cites 9 risks:

– Rip currents
– Shorebreak (when waves break directly on shore)
– Lightning
– Jellyfish
– Heat and sunburn
– Algal blooms
– Water quality
– Marine debris
– Sharks

Generally, the risks of death from jellyfish, algal blooms, water quality and marine debris are minimal, especially since these hazards are monitored by local agencies and warning signs posted if there's an issue. Rip currents and shorebreak present drowning hazards, but the annual risk of death is fairly low (e.g., 1 in 18,000,000), especially if there are lifeguards present. Most people would probably say that sharks are the biggest risk they face when going to the beach. That risk of death is fairly low as well, currently estimated at 1 in 11,500,000. Heat-related injuries and sunburn are very common at the beach, but rarely prove fatal, unless you include sun-induced skin cancers that appear long after the beach visit. The risk of death from lightning is 1 in 10,941,317 that you will be struck and killed. Now consider this: If you are driving a car to the beach, your odds of being killed on the way are around 1 in 42,339. Thus, the most dangerous aspects of going to the beach are: first, the drive to the beach; second, the probability of sunburn and dehydration; and a distant third, the danger of being struck by lightning. So if you're going to the beach, buckle-up, drive safely, put on sunscreen, wear a hat, drink plenty of fluids and find shelter (not under a tall tree!) if it starts to storm. Knowing the facts about the actual risks associated with our activities is key to defining our priorities for making good decisions. **The actual risk statistics often don't align with the "gut" feelings that we have about the risks that we're taking.**

Interpreting risk statistics can be very confusing. Some statistics are offered as "lifetime-odds-of-death" as opposed to "annual-odds-of-death" (**Table 1.**). The average lifetime in the US is about 77 years, so lifetime-odds-of-death will always be much higher (i.e., about 77 times higher) than annual-odds-of-death. **So when using statistical data to com-**

TABLE 1. RISK OF DEATH FROM DIFFERENT CAUSES*

Type of Activity	2020 Deaths	One-Year Odds	Lifetime Odds
Heart Disease	713,347	462	6
Cancer	611,440	539	7
All Preventable Accidents	200,955	1,640	21
Drug Poisoning	83,558	3,943	51
Suicide	45,979	7,166	93
Motor Vehicle Crashes	42,339	7,782	101
Lethal Falls	42,114	7,824	102
Assault	24,576	13,407	174
Medical Complications	5,361	61,459	798
Motorcycle Rider	5,353	61,551	799
Drowning	4,177	78,881	1,024
Fire & Smoke	2,951	111,652	1,450
Alcohol Poisoning	2,665	123,634	1,606
Drowning in Bathtub	642	513,215	6,665
Airplane Crashes	364	905,176	11,756
Hornet, Wasp & Bee Stings	74	4,452,488	57,825
Lightning (2019 data)	30	10,941,317	138,849

*Source: National Center for Health Statistics; National Safety Council

pare risks, be careful to make sure that you're doing an apples-to-apples comparison. The annual risk of being struck and killed by lightning (i.e., 1 in 10,941,317) is a useful statistic to remember since we have an intuitive grasp of how rare that is and thus can serve as a reference point for assessing other risks.

Some activities (like flying on a commercial airliner) have odds that are lower than 1 in 100,000,00. This is an extremely low risk for an activity that many people fear and also be aware that most of the airplane crash fatalities come from **small** airplanes (1 chance in 905,176 of dying). Compare this to failing to be vaccinated during a COVID-19 pandemic, which carries a "crude mortality rate" of about 1 chance in 360 of dying, making this a very risky behavior.

A quick look at **Table 1** reveals many interesting facts. Motor vehicle crashes and lethal falls have a similar probability of ending your life. (Be very careful driving and using ladders, and as my editor will attest, driving behind vehicles carrying ladders.) I also find it shocking that more people die from drug overdoses and suicide than car crashes. Clearly, it is very dangerous to take our mental health for granted and not seek help when we're having problems.

Not surprisingly, cancer and heart disease are the biggest risks that we face. Which leads me neatly to...

Stay Healthy

Any old geezer will tell you that good health is one of the most precious things that you can have. Life is not fun if you're not able to participate in an activity or excursion due to health concerns.

Good health is placed at risk by bad habits like smoking, avoiding check-ups and vaccinations, and doing inverted aerial maneuvers on a snowboard. Be especially careful if engaging in high-impact competitive sports like football. Many folks who were the top football athletes in high school suffered considerable pain that required hip, knee and shoulder replacements later in life.

There is a ton of advice out there for staying healthy, but I am going to try to keep it uncomplicated. My **Three-Step Advice for Good Health** is brief:

Step #1:   Maintain a balanced, healthy diet and get some exercise.
Step #2:   Don't smoke.
Step #3:   If your clothes get too tight, then go to Step #1.

Is this three-step program easy to do? No. Is it essential to leading your life to the fullest? Yes.

Another aspect of healthy living involves regular check-ups and vaccinations. Make sure that your vaccinations are up to date, and your children vaccinated for diphtheria, tetanus, polio, pertussis, human papillomaviruses (HPV), rotavirus, chickenpox, measles, rubella and mumps. Adults who received all of their childhood vaccinations should get a tetanus/diphtheria booster periodically.

Many other available vaccinations for adults could be lifesavers. (Remember, **you need to be vaccinated before being exposed to a disease.** Vaccines can't help you if you already have the disease! Plan accordingly.) Vaccines are available for many diseases, including: influenza, type A & B hepatitis, types A and C meningococcal meningitis, pneumonia, tularemia, rabies, tick fever, shingles and COVID-19. Vaccines are also available for diseases that you might encountered while travelling or in special circumstances, including: adenovirus, anthrax, cholera, rabies, smallpox, typhoid and yellow fever.

When deciding whether to get a specific vaccination, it's best to evaluate your risks of exposure and talk to your doctor about those vaccines that are appropriate for you. You would deeply regret getting a serious case of any of those diseases (or you children getting it) knowing that you failed to get a simple vaccination for it.

Financial Preparedness

We live in a world that requires money to buy the daily necessities of life. It is absolutely true that money cannot buy you love or happiness. But there is something it can buy you: **Some freedom!**

People who develop frugal spending habits early in life usually find themselves under less financial pressure later in life. They can save more and are better able to avoid borrowing a lot of money.

One of the biggest financial decisions that young adults face is educational expense. College tuition costs have risen to ridiculous heights. If you must borrow money to pay the tuition, then you will be saddling yourself with enormous debt before you even have a job. Is it really worth spending $50,000 or more in annual tuition at a prestigious private university when you can get a great education, for much less, at state colleges and community colleges?

If your family has the money to pay for the private school, then great, go for it. If you're going to be financing your own education, then don't even think about the expensive private schools unless you're getting a substantial scholarship. State schools and community colleges today provide excellent educational opportunities at a fraction of the cost of elite private schools. My education at city and state schools was excellent and allowed me to compete with co-workers who graduated from the best schools in the world. **Avoid tuition debt. It is the primary source of financial suffering that young adults endure today.**

There was an old saying, "Go to college and get a high-paying job." This might have been true 60 years ago, but not so much today. Many jobs for recent college grads pay low wages to start, and don't leave much extra money to pay down school loans. Not only that, but there is also a growing trend for companies to require a lower-pay (or even, unpaid) "internship" before they'll even hire you to the low-pay full-time job. The whole situation is immoral, but that's what you're up against in today's times. You have a much better chance for financial independence if you can minimize your student loan debt.

Another strategy is to avoid school loan debt is to forego the college degree and seek training in a trade. Trade school tuitions are more manageable and today the starting salaries can surpass those of college graduates. Also, the advancement opportunities for skilled tradesmen are very good. Many college grads find that they must change jobs regularly in order to get raises in salary. It is true that college graduates can earn more in their lifetimes than trade-school grads, but that differential is evaporating, especially if you are a motivated and competent tradesperson.

Planning for financial independence takes time and effort. We are all exposed to many financial risks ranging from unexpected medical bills, job loss, legal bills, uninsured accidents, etc. **The best way to prepare ourselves for financial risks is to minimize borrowing and have some savings that can act as a cushion in times of emergency.** Saving money takes planning and discipline though, and it is also exceptionally hard to achieve when you are just entering the job market.

As soon as you can, be sure to set up an Individual Retirement Account (IRA) and make annual contributions. Seek out jobs with employers who offer decent health insurance and pensions or 401K investment plans.

As a young person, you probably haven't spent any time thinking about retirement; after all, you just got out of school, so traditional retirement is 50 years away. **Ignoring the prospect of your retirement when you're young is a big mistake.** Now is *exactly* the time to begin saving.

It doesn't need to be a huge amount. Aim to save 5% of every paycheck. If that's fifty bucks out of a one-thousand-dollar check, you'll hardly miss it. But if you can maintain this salary percentage until you're 65, then you'll have a substantial savings. If you have an annual salary of $69,000 (the median US household income, according to 2019 U.S. Census Bureau data) and you start saving 5% at age 25, then that will give you a nest egg of about $531,000 at age 65. If you saved 10% of each paycheck, then you will have $1,062,000.

These calculations assume an annualized return of 6% on your savings. It is true that you might not be making $69,000 at age 25, but your salary is likely to rise substantially over the 40 years that you're working, and it'll average out. You will have some serious bucks saved. In contrast, if you start saving 5% of your paycheck when you're 35, then that will give you a nest egg of $271,000 at age 65. These numbers are a lot smaller, making it quite clear that compound interest over a long period of time is a very powerful wealth-maker. It only really works if you start when you're young!

Besides saving for retirement, it's important to have some savings for a "rainy-day" emergency fund. When you're just out of school, saving for this may not be possible. At some point, when you can periodically add a few bucks to your savings account, aim to have enough money to cover your expenses for three months. Which leads me to another important financial point…

Beware credit cards! These little plastic monsters pose a huge risk to anyone short on cash and unable to control their buying impulses. It is so easy to run up a debt that will crush you financially. While it's important to have at least one (as a means to develop a credit history and to handle small purchases when travelling), be disciplined when using it. Pay off the balance as quickly as you can: The interest rates on these cards are excessive to the point of being immoral. Make the payments on time, because the late fees are a total rip-off.

Debit cards impose better financial discipline since you can't run up any debt. They are a little bit risky because they are like cash: If the card is stolen, then you've lost your money. Stolen credit cards, on the other hand, are indemnified by the credit card company, meaning you are rarely exposed to any charges for any theft or illegal activity.

A number of new financial apps for smartphones make spending and transferring money very easy. These include Zelle, Venmo, Apple Pay, etc. All of these services are different, and you really need to look at the fine print and compare the offerings to figure out which one is best suited for you before you sign up. Apps that make it easier to spend money are risky if you lack self-control. **Whenever you use digital apps for financial transactions, be aware that they increase your exposure to thieves who are constantly coming up with new ways to steal from you.**

Another financial question that frequently comes up is, "Should I arrange a recurring payment for automatic monthly payment?" The answer is "That depends."

If you've got a fat bank account and are not worried about the balance getting so low that you run the risk of an overdraft from an automatic payment, then go for it. Otherwise, just make the on-line payments manually each month. Manual payments also give you an opportunity to review the charges and verify that everything is correct. If you auto-pay your credit card payments, then it might be months before you notice that you've been ripped-off in an identity theft scam.

Driving Your Car: Get Prepared

Perhaps the most common place where all of us encounter significant risk is driving, whether we are the actual driver or a passenger. Some simple questions are useful for self-evaluation:

- Do you have a first-aid kit? Do you know how to use it?
- When driving on trips in the winter, do you keep a blanket and drinking water in the car? How about a candle to keep you warm?
- Did you plan a route in advance, or do you just "wing it" with your smartphone GPS?
- Are the tires in good shape and inflated to the correct pressure?
- Does your flashlight work?
- Do you have jumper cables if your battery dies? Do you know how to use them?
- Do you know where the spare tire and jack are located? Do you know how to change a tire?
- When is the car's next oil change due?
- Where is the registration and proof-of-insurance card?
- Do you know what to do and who to call if you have a wreck?
- What should you do if you encounter heavy fog and low visibility?

Folks who don't have good answers to those questions are not well-prepared drivers. They will have needless difficulties when things go wrong.

This lack of preparedness is in stark contrast to how airplane pilots operate. Pilots follow a specific pre-flight check routine to "kick-the-tires and light-the-fires" before taking off. They determine the route of their flight, study a map and check the enroute weather. They inspect the airplane to make sure that there is nothing obviously wrong with it. Such protocol is essential for their safety, that of any passengers, and for those on the ground along their planned route.

Careful drivers follow a similar routine. They check a map (or an app like Waze or their car's navigation system) for the expected route in order to get a sense of the major roads and directions that they'll be using. They visually inspect the car for any damage or deflated tires before getting into the car. This only takes a minute., and fun fact: Tires are probably the single most important safety concern on an automobile. **Your ability to stop and to maintain control, especially under rainy conditions, is largely dependent on the condition of your vehicle's tires.** Your risks of an accident or injury go up exponentially when you let the tires deteriorate. If you do nothing else to maintain your car, at least keep an eye on the tread wear and inflation.

Be aware **an over-reliance on cell phones for navigation can cause a problem if you don't engage in an overview of the entire route prior to starting your drive.** One young lady that I know was driving home from her out-of-state college for the first time and was using her cell phone map for navigation. As she approached a major city with complicated highway interchanges, her cell phone battery quit, and she had no idea which way to go. She drove around the city, lost for about an hour, before she was able find a store where she could purchase a car charger for the phone. If she had simply reviewed the route before getting into the car, she probably would have been able to find her way home with no difficulty.

How to Handle an "Everyday" Accident Situations

We all have witnessed accidents that happen every day: car crashes, house fires, health emergencies, flooding, storm damage, sporting injuries, etc. We are able to handle most of these by calling 9-1-1, and we prepare for them by purchasing various types of insurance: health insurance, auto insurance, homeowner's insurance, etc. And as you've read in **"Table 1. Risk of death from different causes"**), the risk of being involved in, say, a house fire, is considerably lower than being involved in an automobile accident. So let's discuss what to do if you become involved in an auto accident.

If you have never been involved in an auto accident, then it's probably just a matter of time. Fortunately most involve minor injuries, but even then, the damages to the cars can be substantial. (We'll get to the all-important emergency medical preparedness later in this chapter.) And it can be really hard to deal with an accident if you've been shaken up by the experience. So it's not a bad idea to **keep a Six-Point Accident Checklist in your car so that you won't forget to do these six specific things in any accident situation:**

1) Stay safe. Move your vehicle off the road if it's safe to drive. Call 911 to report the accident and any injuries to you or the other person.
2) Get the other driver's contact info (i.e., name, address, license plate number, email/telephone info and insurance company).
3) If there are witnesses who stop, then collect their contact information as well to avoid disputes in the account of what actually occurred.
4) Take photographs of the cars (including damage to both your vehicle and theirs) and people involved.
5) Remain at the scene until the police arrive. The police report will be important to the insurance companies.
6) **Don't admit fault or sign any papers.** Leave that for the insurance companies.

Depending on the amount of damage, then you may (or may not) want to call the insurance company to file a claim. If the damage is minor and your insurance policy has a $1,000 deductible for the collision insurance, then it may be a better idea to simply pay for the repairs out-of-pocket since your insurance premiums will probably be increased as a result of the accident claim, and you'll still need to pay the first $1,000 out-of-pocket.

While we're on the subject of auto insurance, how much insurance should you have? Most states set minimum limits for liability insurance. It always a good idea to carry more than the minimum, but the amount depends on your financial situation. In 2022, most insurance agents will recommend a policy that provides at least $100K of injury liability per person, $300K of injury liability per accident, and $100K of property damage coverage. You may also want to consider adding comprehensive coverage for collision damage and other hazards. **As you get older and accumulate more assets, then you would be wise to increase your coverage to minimize your personal financial exposure in an accident-related lawsuit.**

Similar to car wrecks, the response to sporting accidents, house fires, health emergencies and other everyday accidents is pretty much the same: Dial 9-1-1.

The main difference will be who responds to the call (e.g., a tow truck, a police car, an ambulance or a fire truck, or all four).

We can usually take comfort in the knowledge that our local government has done a reasonably good job preparing for everyday emergencies and can take care of us.

How to Handle a "WTSHTF" Accident Situation

Most young people have never considered the full range of emergencies that they might encounter during their lives. So at this point it is appropriate to **explore other types of serious emergencies that rarely happen, but for which there will be no response when you dial 9-1-1.** The phone will be dead. In these times, your personal preparedness will be decisive to your survival.

We're talking about the low-probability but devastating **"WTSHTF"** (**"When The Sh*t-Hits-The-Fan"**) emergencies. These types of emergencies include nuclear fallout from a war, reactor accident, and/or terrorist incident. They include pandemics, climate-related disasters, food shortages (as in what has been happening right now in terms of baby formula supply, for example), super-volcanoes, tsunamis, meteor impacts, and/or long-duration disruption of public gas, electricity, water utilities, and so forth. Should we prepare for those? Surely the government has a plan to deal with all that. Is that not what FEMA (Federal Emergency Management Agency) is for? Unfortunately, in a significant wide-scale emergency, FEMA has been and will be overwhelmed.

It was on August 23, 2005, that a tropical cyclone named "Hurricane Katrina" slammed into the Gulf Coast and caused massive damage along with the loss of 1,800 lives. But it wasn't until September 2nd that military relief crews were on the scene, and the floodwaters weren't pumped out until October 11. This was a catastrophic event whose damage was mainly localized to the city of New Orleans, and yet the best efforts of FEMA and the U.S. government left the residents almost entirely on their own for 2 weeks, and crippled for almost 2 months. **Clearly, any emergency plan created for a catastrophic situation that depends on the immediate assistance of others is flawed. We need to be able to take care of ourselves and immediate families in disaster-type situations.**

What are the unusual, less-frequent catastrophic threats that we face? The list is longer than you might think:

1) Climate-related disasters
   (e.g., hurricanes, tornados, hurricanes, flooding, drought, wild fires).

2) Infrequent natural phenomena
   (e.g., earthquakes, volcanoes, super-volcanoes, tsunamis, meteor and asteroid impacts, pandemics).

3) Conflict-related disasters
   (e.g., war, chemical, biological and/or nuclear terrorist attacks,

4) Infrastructure failure
   (e.g., electricity, water, or natural gas supply failures)

Common to all of these disasters is the disruption of supply lines. When this occurs, food, clean water, electricity and fuel will not be readily available. Fire, police and medical services may not be readily available. Our normal shelter may have been destroyed or flooded. How long could you get by without the normal sources of food, clean water, electricity and fuel? Preparedness gives us the means to make-do for the time that it is likely to take help to arrive.

The recent COVID-19 pandemic has made us all keenly aware of the possibility of crisis-induced supply interruptions. Most of us already think about hurricanes and tornados as real threats and have made some modest preparations (e.g., flashlights, batteries, bottled water and canned soup) for these events. Increasingly, we are beginning to understand the profound impact of climate change on the world as we experience more powerful storms, more frequent storms, more flooding, more drought, and more severe fires.

Three Things You Cannot Live Without

Out of all these threats, one thing is certain: We need to prepare ourselves for more frequent climate-related supply interruptions. **Survival experts will tell you that the three things that we need most in emergencies are clean air, clean water and food.**

The "Rule-of-Threes" tells us that we can't survive without:

1) clean air for more than **three minutes**
2) clean water for more than **three days**
3) food for more than **three weeks**

What does this tell us? Air is more important than water, and water is more important than food.

Always Have a Way to Get **Clean Air**

Fortunately, there are relatively few scenarios that would deprive us of clean air. Perhaps the worst would be a radioactive fallout event or proximity to a volcanic eruption. Industrial chemical accidents or chemical terrorist attacks could also result in breathing air contamination, but generally, these incidents would be highly localized and difficult to prepare for, since effective gas masks need filters that are specific to the toxic gas that has been released. (However, if you live next to a chemical plant producing chlorine, then it would not be crazy to have gas masks with chlorine filters available to your family.)

Dealing with air contamination from nuclear fallout can be straight-forward if you have a shelter space that will provide protection against radiation and a fan-driven (HEPA) High Efficiency Particulate Air-filter to remove radioactive dust from the air supplied to the shelter. HEPA filters are able to remove 99.97% of all particles that are 0.3 microns in size and larger. This is very, very clean. (More on this later.)

Always Have a Way to Get Clean Water

We can survive without food for a few weeks, but we really need water, especially if we're under stress. **Preparing for an emergency supply of clean water is our single most important priority.** We need to prepare for scenarios where we "shelter-in-place" (i.e., stay in our homes) as well as scenarios where we are "on-the-move" (e.g., for an evacuation). Both require different strategies and equipment.

To "shelter-in-place," we need about 1 to 2 gallons of water, per person, per day, for drinking and sanitation. (This minimal amount stands in stark contrast to the average 80 to 100 gallons per person that we typically use in our homes on non-emergency days.) If we assume a family of four is needing emergency water for 4 weeks, then this translates into 112 to 224 gallons.

This quantity is not too difficult to achieve if you consider using the water stored in your household hot-water heater (typically 50 to 75 gallons) and if you have one or more bathtubs (typically 50 to 100 gallons) that can be filled with water in anticipation of an emergency. FYI, the cleanliness of stored bathtub water is greatly enhanced with the use of a sealed, plastic storage liner (available commercially). Another option is a plastic water storage tank kept in a closet, garage or basement space. These are commonly available in a variety of sizes and are not too expensive. They can easily provide a few weeks of reliable drinking water.

Be aware that the majority of FEMA emergency planning is focused on evacuation. This will place us "on-the-move." When we are "on-the-move," our water requirements are basically the same, but transporting 150 gallons of water (weighing about 1250 pounds) is not usually an option. So when "on-the-move," we need to be able to use water of unknown purity that we find along the way. This water may be from a well, or surface water from a river, lake, pond or rain puddle. Or it could be water being supplied from a good Samaritan that just doesn't look and smell right.

The main water contaminants that we need to guard against are microorganisms and toxic chemicals. These need to be removed before we can drink water from any unknown or sketchy source.

Microorganism-contaminated Water

There are four main ways to eliminate microorganisms and other living pathogens from drinking water in emergency situations. These include:

1) Filtration
2) Ultraviolet (UV) sterilization
3) Chemical treatment
4) Heat treatment (i.e., boiling)

Filtration involves passing the water through holes (e.g., 0.2 microns in diameter) that are big enough to let water molecules through but too small to allow microorganisms to pass. There are a variety of popular filter media available today. **Some of the best use microporous ceramics that are sometimes impregnated with silver (e.g., Katadyn, Berkey etc.).** These modern filters can be used immediately, and most can be cleaned for re-use. They are either gravity-fed or hand-pumped and come in a range of sizes from pocket-sized filters for one person to filters for large groups of people. These water filters are among the most important gear that we should all have for an emergency. While these filters do handle the most commonly found water-borne pathogens, be aware there are viruses and some less-common bacteria that can pass through the filter. (but these usually represent a minor risk.)

A fairly new, alternative approach to dealing with microorganism-contaminated drinking water is UV sterilization. UV sterilizer widgets are available as a battery-powered, pocket-sized device (e.g., Steri-Pen) that does not kill the microorganisms, but rather renders them incapable of reproducing as a result of UV radiation damage to their DNA. These devices work in less than a minute and are really handy when travelling to destinations that have questionable water quality. The UV sterilizers are more effective than filtration systems if viruses are present in the water. Just make sure that you have spare batteries on hand.

Chemical treatment purifies water by adding a chemical (typically a powerful oxidizing agent like chlorine, bleach, or hypochlorous acid) that kill the microorganisms by denaturing the proteins in the microorganism. **Purification tablets come in many forms (e.g., "Halazone" and Sodium DiChloroisoCyanurate "NaDCC") and are commonly used in water disinfection.** These tablets are simple to use, effective and inexpensive, but you must wait up to several hours for the chemical treatment to work. They also leave the water with an undesirable aftertaste.

The traditional method for eliminating pathogens from drinking water is boiling. This is also simple and effective but requires fuel and time. During an emergency, fuel might be unavailable. Boiling is inconvenient when "on-the-move".

An ideal strategy for dealing with microorganism-contaminated water is to equip yourself with gear to apply all four approaches. All of these approaches are great for removing microorganisms from water, although they are **not** effective for removing toxic chemicals.

Chemically-contaminated Water

Fortunately, chemically-contaminated water is less likely to be a problem (when compared to water-borne pathogens). Chemical contaminants can be produced by a wide range of sources, but the major ones are: heavy metals (e.g., lead and arsenic from wells or old corroded water pipes);

fuels and solvents (e.g., gasoline, oil, paint thinner, etc. from automotive and industrial activities); and agricultural run-off (e.g., fertilizers, pesticides and herbicides). **All of these chemicals can be efficiently removed from drinking water by using a granulated activated charcoal ("GAC") filter.**

Granulated activated charcoal is an amazing material, having an enormous number of molecularly sized pores that trap a broad range of metals and organic chemicals. "GAC" filters are the heart of popular "Brita" and "Pur" home water filters. They are great at removing chemicals but not useful for removing microorganisms.

A Recommended Clean-Water Preparedness Strategy

Stock-piling some clean water that will satisfy our minimal needs for a few days is the easiest thing that we can do, but we also need to be prepared to produce clean water when the stockpile runs out, or if we need to be "on-the-move" for an evacuation.

For reliably clean water, we need:

1) Either a gravity-fed or hand-pumped microporous membrane filter to eliminate microorganisms from alternative water sources. (The hand-held UV sterilizers are great, but they require batteries that might not be available.)
2) A "GAC" filter to eliminate toxic chemicals.

Some of the microporous membrane filters for microorganisms also contain activated charcoal filtration elements (e.g., Berkey), so shop around for devices that have a capacity to meet your expected water requirements and that are proven effective for removing both microorganisms and toxic chemicals.

Where is the Food?

Meeting our food needs in an emergency requires some planning. There are two scenarios we need to consider:

1) Short-term emergency (i.e., less than 2 weeks)
2) Long-term emergency (i.e., more than 6 months)

In the Short-Term

We should all be prepared to handle short-term food emergencies. This can be done by simply stocking our pantries with more non-perishable foods that we normally eat and rotating through them when we prepare regular meals. It's not too expensive to do this, although it requires a bit more management of the food inventory (this is doable by most families). **A thoughtfully over-stocked pantry is really all that you need for short-term emergencies.**

Over the Long Term

Preparing for a long-term food emergency takes more planning and may require a financial investment that is more than many families are willing to commit. Generally speaking, long-term food supplies require a combination of different approaches. These include freeze-dried foods stored in sealed containers, retort-packaged foods (e.g., MRE "Meals-Ready-to-Eat"), canned meats and vegetables, and grains and beans stored in sealed, airtight containers with oxygen scavengers. The shelf life of these foods varies. Most manufacturers are comfortable guaranteeing a 5-year shelf life, but anecdotal reports suggest that if stored in a cool place, these foods can remain tasty for 15 to 20 years. Cooking oils though are a problem for long-term storage since most turn rancid after a couple of years.

Emergency Cash Needs

Do we need old-fashioned cash during an emergency? Absolutely.

In 1989 a magnitude 6.9 earthquake hit Loma Prieta on California's central coast. Dozens died and thousands were injured. It was called the "World Series Earthquake" because it shook Candlestick Park in San Francisco on live TV when the San Francisco Giants and Oakland Athletics were about to begin playing. I had occasion to visit that part of the country a few weeks after the event and asked my friends what they would do differently regarding preparing for earthquakes. I found out most had already stocked some water and food, and that some had generators. Everyone said that the thing they hadn't considered was the fact that the extended power outages would make it impossible to use credit cards to buy gas or anything else at the local stores for almost a week. They all said they wished that they had more cash on hand after the earthquake. (Be prepared!)

Does Long-Term Emergency Preparedness Make Any Sense?

What could cause a long-term emergency where food and supplies would be scarce or largely unavailable for more than 6 months? Here is a short list:

1) Nuclear war
2) Large asteroid or meteor impact
3) Super-volcano eruption

Many folks will read that list and laugh at how preposterous these threats seem:

- "Large asteroid or meteor impact? You've got to be kidding! Nothing like that has happened in 10,000 years. I'll be dead long before that happens again."

- "Super-volcano! What have you been smoking? Nobody's ever seen one of those."
- "We've managed to avoid nuclear war for more than 70 years. Surely the global nuclear powers would never be stupid enough to actually use the weapons, right?"

Such skepticism is entirely valid. But if there is anything on this planet that *could* result in a "WTSHTF" global emergency, those are the most likely culprits.

It is important to remind ourselves that the earth has been evolving for over 4 billion years. Large asteroid impacts have occurred countless times during the earth's history and will continue to occur. An asteroid impact 66 million years ago extinguished the dinosaurs and 75% of all other living species on earth. We are just beginning to develop technology to detect and predict these impacts as well as (perhaps) nudge their trajectories to avoid a collision with the earth. Even if we get this technology fully developed, there will still be devastating asteroid impacts on earth in the future. Is it a near-term threat? Probably not. Is it a survivable threat? Absolutely, if you're prepared and not in the immediate impact zone. With human technology to store and preserve food for extended periods of time, it is certainly possible for a significant number of humans to survive the type of asteroid impact that wiped out the dinosaurs—if they are prepared.

Volcanic activity continues on earth today. Big volcanos can have lasting effects on global climate beyond their localized devastation. A well-documented super-volcano located in Yellowstone Park has erupted with some regularity about every 650,000 years, and its last major eruption occurred about 640,000 years ago. So when this baby blows again, it's going to bury the heartland of America under ash. Is it a near-term threat? Probably not. Is it a survivable threat? Absolutely, if you're prepared and not in the immediate blast zone.

In terms of a global nuclear war, most of us will find little comfort in knowing that the primary thing that stands in its way war is the wisdom, peaceful intentions, and deep compassion of our world leaders (some of whom, you might recall, are crazy, murderous, dirt-bag dictators). A global nuclear war would disable most of the important infrastructure that is needed to grow food and deliver it.

Any blasts from nuclear weapons are devastating, but localized. This means if you're within a mile or two of a 100 kilo-ton blast, you're toast. And even if the blast over-pressure doesn't get you, then the huge radiation flux will. Matter near the blast zone will be made radioactive by activation from the massive neutron flux produced in the fission reaction.

For the majority of us, the real problem is radioactive fallout. Radioactive fallout would require the survivors around the globe to seek shelter for months until the radiation levels subsided. It is likely that an entire food-growing season would be lost, and anything that did grow might be heavily contaminated with radioactive fallout. It is also a possibility that so much dust would be delivered into the upper atmosphere that the earth would be darkened during a "nuclear winter" that would last a year or more. Thus, it might require sheltering and relying on emergency supplies for two years to truly survive a global nuclear war.

The most likely threat to our survival from a global nuclear war is the nuclear fallout, and there are survivalists who feel a moral imperative to try to survive any cataclysmic event, believing it is their duty to the human race to try to carry on, especially if the majority of people on earth have been killed. Many folks who are not survivalists per se still see the value in preparing for long-term emergencies, including members of the Church of Jesus Christ of Latter-day Saints (i.e., Mormons), who are encouraged to maintain at least a 3-month supply of food in their household. Many Mormon households are stocked with a 1-year supply.

Switzerland mandated fallout shelter construction in all new buildings since 1978. The Swiss now have enough fallout shelters to accommodate 110% of the population of their country. Sweden has shelters for 81% of its population. It is difficult to find information on the percentage of the US population that has immediate access to viable fallout shelters. It's doubtful that the US has viable shelters for even 5% of the civilian population.

Back in the 1960s the U.S. had an ambitious civil defense program to identify, mark and stock buildings, subways, mines, caves and any other structure that could serve as fallout shelters. (You might be surprised to read I worked in this program as a certified "Fallout Shelter Survey Technician" with the US Army Corps of Engineers.) Unfortunately this civil defense program was phased out at the end of the Cold War and all of the shelters and associated supplies were forgotten.

Today the "duck-and-cover" civil defense campaign of the 1960's is widely mocked as a cheesy public-relations Band-Aid. While it is true that very few of these shelters could provide nuclear blast protection, they were still very useful to escape the radioactive fallout that is the major hazard of a nuclear war.

The majority of Americans currently believe that nuclear war is unthinkable, and so they don't think about the possibility. But I'm here to let you know that while the U.S. government actively maintains incredibly sophisticated, up-to-date bunkers for itself, its citizens will be protected by... FEMA.

CartoonStock.com

If you too have concerns about FEMA's ability to offer meaningful protection to nuclear fallout (remember: Hurricane Katrina), then you might consider building your own fallout shelter.

Fallout Shelter Construction

Basically the objective will be to put as much mass (i.e., matter of any kind) as possible between you and the sources of radiation. Radioactive fallout will rain down as dust particles on the roof of your house and on the ground around the house, with the primary threat being from gamma radiation whose energetic photons travel in straight lines. Thus, basements are the best places to build fallout shelters since they're already protected by a large mass of earth on five sides.

The gold standard for a useful fallout shelter aims to provide a protection-factor (i.e., "PF") of 1000. That means that radiation on the outside of the shelter will be reduced by a factor of 1000x inside the shelter. This much attenuation of gamma radiation is achievable with 24 inches of reinforced concrete. It is tough to add a 24" reinforced concrete basement ceiling to an existing home, so even 12" would be good (providing a PF = 32), but still very tough to do. As a result, **it's best to consider constructing a protective fallout shelter when a new home is being designed.**

Adding the requisite 24" reinforced concrete walls and ceiling will add a somewhat modest incremental cost to the home (approx. $10K as of this writing), especially if a basement is already being planned.

Any shelter space does not need to be very large, with FEMA recommending a minimum of 10 square feet per occupant. I believe this is pretty tight; 40 square feet seems preferable. It is hard for me to imagine spending 2 months in my 200 square-foot shelter with more than 6 people.

The benefits of having such a shelter go beyond that of avoiding fallout. The space can be used as a general-purpose "safe room" that will provide peace of mind during other, more frequent and less-severe, emergency weather situations such as tornadoes, hurricanes, etc. It's also useful as a man cave (or, so as not to be old-fashioned or chauvinistic, a she-shed) when you need a quiet place for a high-stakes poker game with "bunker-beer" or other locally distilled alcoholic beverages on tap.

If you have an existing home without a basement, then the best option is to dig a hole in the back yard and install a prefab shelter into the ground. This is more expensive and less convenient than a "safe-room" inside your home, but it will provide excellent radiation and tornado protection.

One additional consideration that is critically important is **ventilation**. The shelter probably won't require any heat because of the natural heat generated by the occupants. Having an adequate ventilation system to remove that heat and supply fresh air is very important. The powered (human or electric) air delivery system must be equipped with a large High Efficiency Particulate Air (HEPA) filter so that radioactive dust particles (and as a bonus, biological pathogens) will be filtered from the breathing air that is being brought inside the shelter.

Don't forget to stock-up on potassium iodide (KI) tablets in the shelter. Nuclear fallout often contains high concentrations of radioactive iodine that collects in the thyroid gland. Taking KI tablets prophylactically during a nuclear emergency will load up the thyroid with non-radioactive iodine to prevent thyroid damage.

There is a long list of additional considerations (e.g., electrical power, lighting, toilets, water supply, sleeping space, radios, medical supplies, radiation meters, etc.) that need to be considered in any practical fallout shelter; the "Crisis Preparedness Handbook" by Jack Spigarelli is a good place to start.

For technical info on fallout shelters check out "Design Guidance for Shelters and Safe Rooms", *FEMA Risk Management Series,* Document 453.

How Much Effort Should I Spend on Emergency Preparedness?

Emergency preparedness is a type of self-insurance: It provides coverage for situations that regular insurance policies cannot handle. And so like with any insurance policy, you need to know two things: what situations do you want to cover, and how much coverage do you want?

Some of us can afford some insurance and some of us can't. The approach that I've always taken is to calculate the amount that I spend each year on car, home, life and health insurance premiums, and allocate a percentage of that to my personal "WTSHTF" insurance plan. (In my case, that allocation usually was in the range of 5% to 10%.) This can amount to a significant investment over a 20-year period, easily permitting the purchase of water purification equipment, year-long food supplies for the entire family, and even a modest fallout shelter.

All emergency preparedness strategies should aim for a continuous investment over a period of time. (It's hard to do it all in one step). Here is a simple plan to consider:

1) Get a water-purification device first.
2) Improve your pantry stocks to give you a few weeks of food and water independence.

After you've worked your way through these two steps, carefully consider the specific threats that you face in the specific place that you live and plan accordingly. **The important thing is to realize that you cannot depend solely on other people (e.g., FEMA) to come immediately to save you in a disaster. Recognize that you and your family will be completely on your own initially.**

Be prepared to take care of yourselves.

Emergency Communications

Whenever I'm travelling or engaged in any outdoor activity, I always bring a communication device. Doing so is actually more important than carrying matches, Band-Aids or a Swiss Army knife. You don't need anything more for emergency preparedness if you know that when you call for help, that someone will answer the call and respond quickly.

The choice of communication device though is really important. If I'm in an area that I am certain has good cellphone coverage, then I just make sure that my cellphone is adequately charged before beginning my activity. But when I'm doing wilderness activities, I am aware the probability of reliable cellphone coverage is usually poor. For instance, relying solely on a cellphone for emergency assistance is very risky if you or the person with you (you are out in the wilderness with someone else, right?) happen to injure yourself in a cellphone dead-spot and you are unable to climb up to a point where you have a signal. Most people grossly over-estimate the reliability of cellphone service when out of town, on a boat, or on a ski slope, and they can get into big trouble when they have an emergency and can't get a signal.

A few decades ago, there were very few options to deal with the wilderness emergency communication problem. As a nerdy ham radio operator, I would sometimes carry a small battery-powered 2m VHF FM radio transceiver, but these (like cellphones) required a favorable location for them to be able to hit a repeater 20 or 30 miles away and be heard by another ham. Ultimately, the best thing that you could do back then was to let multiple people know about your travel intentions and tell them when you expected to return. If they didn't hear from you at the appointed date and time, then they were instructed to call for a search party. (This is still a good thing to do.)

Today, we have available to us small, pocket-sized communication devices that monitor our exact location via GPS and, at the push of an SOS button, summon help immediately via a network of satellite repeaters. For families, these are probably one of the most important pieces of safety equipment that you can own, as they work anywhere on this planet.

The Garmin InReach Mini and Spot Gen4 are two of these popular devices, and they use the Iridium and Globalstar satellite constellations. They also have a built-in GPS that permit those who carry them to send non-SOS messages from one unit to another. Both small and water-resistant, they don't even need to be turned on until there is an emergency, so battery life is not a big issue. In a "WTSHTF" emergency, the internet and cellphone systems will be jammed and/or non-functional, but these satellite-based communicators should still be able to operate.

These devices should be standard equipment in everyone's car when travelling and in the pocket when hiking, skiing, boating, canoeing, etc. In a serious emergency when phones and internet are down, these devices will allow family members (who are possibly scattered in different locations) to have a means to coordinate their plans to rendezvous.

Gun Safety

Growing up in New York City in the previous century, the only people I knew who had guns were policemen, gangsters, or the occasional hunter. Very few people even thought about owning guns for their personal protection. Today the situation is quite different, with guns abundant in the USA. It's hard to know exactly how many, but the number is believed to be about 400,000,000… indicating there are more guns than people in the USA.

This proliferation of guns poses a dilemma for citizens who strongly support gun control or outright bans on firearms. If they don't own a gun, then they are seriously outgunned by some of their neighbors. This is a serious concern for anyone interested in emergency preparedness. If an emergency situation gets really bad and people become desperate, then it may be necessary to protect yourself. Having a gun and ammunition could be critical to your survival.

Hoping for this gun-craziness to subside is wishful thinking. The government is unlikely to outlaw firearms due to the 2nd Amendment (the right to bear arms). Banning "military assault weapons" might be a good public-relations gesture but it won't do much to actually reduce the firearm threat. With about 20,000,000 AR15 and AK47 style assault rifles out there right now, even an enormously successful campaign to confiscate them would be lucky to get 90% of that number… and that still leaves 2,000,000 assault rifles "on-the-street." Besides, a vastly greater number of deadly hunting rifles and handguns would still be available.

The gun genie is out-of-the-bottle and she's not going back in.

Considering all of these factors, owning a gun and learning how to use it safely and properly makes a lot of sense. The majority of gun owners are responsible people, and you can be too even if you've never held one in your hands.

The best way to learn is to get some instruction on the use and care of a firearm. Go to a range, take a class and practice so that you know how your gun works and know that you can use it safely. However, also understand that **running away is always the best action (if possible) in an armed confrontation.** If you are a gunowner, get a gun-safe and keep it locked up when you're not using it. We don't live in the wild west, but if a bad situation presents itself, then you will have options with a firearm that could save your life. (Besides, shooting targets and sporting clays is a lot of fun!)

Medical Emergency Preparedness

Speaking of disasters, bad situations and accidents, these are often accompanied by physical injuries. We all need to be prepared to offer first aid, both to ourselves and to others. That means it's always good to have Band-Aids and antibiotic crèmes available for routine cuts and scrapes.

Keeping an emergency supply of prescription drugs on hand is not practical or doable, unless you are a physician. However, many prescription drugs (especially antibiotics) are available via mail-order on a non-prescription basis for animal (e.g., pet fish & bird) use. **It is often the case that these antibiotics are identical to those manufactured for human consumption.** Consider maintaining a stockpile (e.g., Cephalexin, Amoxicillin, Ciprofloxacin, Metronidazole and Azithromycin) of these as part of your emergency preparedness planning.

There are two very useful books I'd like to recommend to help you develop medical preparedness. The authors of each are Joseph Alton, MD and Amy Alton ARNP. The first book (written for the layman) is, "The Survival Medicine Handbook: A Guide for When Help is NOT on the Way," and its companion book, "Alton's Antibiotics and Infectious Disease: The Layman's Guide to Available Antibacterials in Austere Settings" offers great advice on selecting and obtaining antibiotics for preparedness purposes.

The most important element of medical emergency preparedness is **training,** however. Having extensive supplies is meaningless if you don't know how to use them. **Medical emergency preparedness requires at least a course in basic first aid and CPR.** Also know how to perform the Heimlich Maneuver. Seek out local organizations such as the Red Cross and YMCA, which usually and frequently offer first-aid training.

Share Any Emergency Preparedness Plans with the Family

Whatever emergency preparations you decide to make, it is important to share information about your preparations with your immediate family members who are living with you. Sit them down and explain what preparations (e.g., designated saferoom, supplies, fire extinguishers, etc.) you've made and how to access them. Describe the scenarios in which these preparations might be necessary. It is also useful to discuss the **limitations of** those preparations and those scenarios with which you are not prepared to deal.

Create and share a file later on with everyone's phone number and email address so that you can re-connect if you don't have access to your cellphone or computer. Also designate an out-of-town relative or friend that you will use as a contact point if you need to evacuate and end up getting separated. Include their contact information on the list.

And above all, don't forget to develop **a fire emergency plan** for your home. Determine the best escape routes from each room, and the locations of the fire extinguishers and water hoses that can be used to suppress a fire that has just started.

Make sure that you have fire extinguishers handy near places where fires might start, especially near the kitchen. The type of extinguisher suitable for a kitchen fire typically would be rated for type A, B & C fires, and weigh at least 5 pounds.

Be sure to check any fire extinguishers periodically to make sure that they are still "charged," ensure that everyone knows how to use a fire extinguisher. Most fires start small and if you work to extinguish them quickly, you can be prevented major damage.

Verify that the windows that you might use for escape (the ones in a bedroom or by the kitchen, for example) can open easily. If you have a security system with a fire-call button, then make sure that everyone knows where they are and how to activate them. **It's very important to establish a rendezvous point outside the house so that everyone will go there once they get out of the home, making it possible to quickly figure out who is still in the house.**

Chapter 7.

Get Hired, Not Fired: Job Success Tips

In many cases personal financial success and a sense of self-worth are deeply entwined with job success, making how we do at our professions critically important.

Finding a job, and finding *the* right job, can be difficult or easy, although there are also plenty of opportunities (depending on the current state of the economy). Available jobs come from many organizations:

a.bacall

"You're exactly the kind of applicant we're looking for."

perhaps a small business, large public corporation, school, church, government, or a non-profit charity organization. All these organizations expect certain skills and competence from their employees, and our mastery of those skills is important to getting hired as well as our ultimate occupational success.

How to Get Hired

Getting hired can be really tough and discouraging. This is especially true if you are just out of school, or over the age of 50 and looking for a new job. Finding a job requires that you employ every tool at your disposal, including on-line job clearinghouses, networking sites, professional societies, personal friends, school job placement offices, and so forth.

The internet offers a variety of excellent on-line sites (e.g., www.indeed.com, www.ziprecruiter.com, www.productopia.com, etc.) that serve as clearinghouses for job placements. They are certainly the first place worth exploring when you're on the job market.

There are also many good ways to network on-line. Consider joining Linkedin. If you have a degree and there are professional societies associated with your field, join the respective societies and take advantage of the job clearinghouse and networking opportunities they offer.

I've had many great jobs over the years (I'm an old-geezer Boomer Dad after all) and, with the exception of a couple of US Government temporary job positions, I've never been hired for any job that I applied for. **Every job that I've been hired to do has been the result of a personal contact who knew my abilities and made a connection for me.** Lacking any family connections, personal networking was the most important factor for me to get a job. The network connections came from folks that I went to school with, or teachers and professors who knew me. They would sometimes be approached by companies looking for specific skills and they'd connect the students with the companies looking for new hires.

"Well, YOU tell personnel you need every
winter off and see if you get a job!"

CartoonStock.com

Employment agencies (or "Head-Hunters," as they are sometimes called) can provide connections when your personal contacts are limited or not yielding any prospects. It is often the case that taking a job as a temporary worker can turn into a permanent job if it turns out you are a good fit for the company.

When you do get asked to interview, be sure to prepare for it. Here are a few specific tips:

- Be punctual and neatly groomed. Don't be late; don't be too early. If you are more than 5 minutes early, then kill some time before you enter the building. It's not good to be too early because interviewers are often busy and not ready to see you until the scheduled time.

113

- Learn as much as you can about the company, its products, the people who will be interviewing you, and the specific job that you're seeking.
- Practice answers to common interview questions such as, Why do you want to work here? What salary are you expecting? What is the specific area in which you need the most improvement? What job experience did you wish you had done differently? Tell me about yourself.
- When the interview begins, sit up straight, take a deep breath and **smile.**
- Answer any questions honestly. Be positive. Avoid dissing your previous employers. Don't ramble. Keep your answers concise and to-the-point.
- Be prepared to talk about **specific skills that you have that align with the job description.**
- Be sure to ask questions about the day-to-day responsibilities of the job, how job performance is measured, if regular travel is required, and so forth.
- During the interview process it is important for you to learn whether the job is full-time and what specific benefits are provided. Some companies are deceptive in their advertising for a position, and it is only at the interview that, with the proper questioning, you may discover they are only offering reduced working hours that lie below the threshold where by law they must provide the employee with "full-time" benefits (like health insurance).
- Ask about advancement opportunities that might be available to you.

Fundamental Job Skills

When you are hired, businesses expect you to have many of the desirable "personal traits" described in chapter 2, plus additional skills. Whether your chosen occupation is to be a ditch digger, an electrician, a McDonald's worker, a CMO, or an entrepreneur, there are some basic things that every worker, whatever their occupation, must master to be as successful as possible in their jobs:

1) **Show Up.** Showing-up for work *punctually* is really important. Show up on time and leave only after your day or shift is complete. Don't sneak in late and leave early; co-workers and clients might be counting on you being there to assist them, and it won't go over well if your supervisor finds out about the shenanigans.
   If there's a specific reason you can't show up on time one time, then let someone know that you'll be late. It's important to be dependable and act like a trustworthy member of the team.

2) **Pay Attention.** Aim to be a "quick study "when being trained for a new job. Engage. Listen. Ask good questions. Make notes. Show enthusiasm. It will be noticed.

3) **Do a Quality Job.** An old proverb says, "If it's worth doing, then it's worth doing well." Don't cut corners. Most businesses are keenly aware of the importance of quality within the organization, and within the quality of products that they sell.
   The core principle of all quality systems is "to do what you say that you are going to do." Your word is your bond, so if you accept a task and are having problems completing it, then get help. Let someone know that there is a problem, as you should completely finish any project that you're doing. If the product you're delivering doesn't meet your own standards, then don't pass it to a customer. Make sure things are done and created right

4) **Know the Rules and Follow the Rules.** All companies have policies and procedures regarding employee behavior, dress codes, vacation leave, etc. Familiarize yourself with the employee handbook. Being familiar with the policies and procedures and following the rules demonstrates to management that you are a diligent, trustworthy employee... one who should be promoted one day if the opportunity arises.

Becoming a "Professional"

If your ambition is taking you in the direction of "professional" jobs, then the necessary skills you are to display are more difficult, but the salaries which compensate you for those skills will be higher than those offered for many blue-collar jobs. The term "professional" refers to folks who earn their living by doing an activity that requires a certain level of education, skill, or training. Some professionals (e.g., physicians, nurses, lawyers, accountants, architects, professional engineers, airline pilots, etc.) are required to have their proficiency licensed or certified by an independent accrediting group.

"Professionals" also are often required to work outside of the "normal" 9 to 5 working hours. They are often tethered to work by cellphones, text messaging and email. They many have unpredictable schedules based on the specific deadline requirements of their clients. Most professionals work hard but enjoy higher-than-average pay along with the satisfaction of doing work that has noticeable impact. The downside here is that professional jobs can be stressful and time-consuming.

Develop Inter-Disciplinary Skills

Many people think that specialization is the key to a successful career. This can be true if there is a specialized job that needs your specialized skills. Many jobs are less specialized, requiring a range of skills to be effective. This is especially true in small businesses where employees sometimes need to "wear multiple hats" in order to get the job done. Is it better to be a narrowly trained specialist or a broadly trained generalist? Both paths can lead to successful careers. Choosing the right path for you requires some careful introspection.

In college I came to realize that many interesting problems were at the interfaces of several different specialized disciplines (e.g., biology, chemistry and physics). This led me to pursue a generalist strategy.

A **generalist** is the person you need when doing pioneering exploration. For example, a generalist pioneer-explorer in Africa will speak enough Swahili, English, Bantu, and perhaps French to get around successfully. The generalist will never write a great novel in any of those languages but will be able to effectively interact with the people in that region.

My desire to explore new frontiers lead me to pursue formal training in engineering and chemistry. This enabled me to "speak the language" of the associated specialists, allowing me to solve problems that would have challenged a larger team of specialists.

Climbing the Corporate Ladder

Depending on your personal ambitions, you might want to seek promotions within your workplace. Achieving higher levels of responsibility and pay level can be very satisfying. Some companies have well-defined paths to promotions. Talk to your supervisor and ask for advice on how to get promotions within the organization and what to expect.

Many other organizations do not have well defined paths to promotions, or present a situation where there are many viable candidates in line ahead of you. It is a common experience today to find yourself two or three years into a new job, receiving praise for your hard work, and with little or no prospect for promotion. Often, the only path to a promotion and higher salary is to quit your job and find a new one where your experience will allow your starting salary to be higher.

In Boomer-Dad's-day it was not unusual for folks to take a job right out of school and retire from that same organization 35 years later. That is very rare today. Instead, it is often necessary to "job-hop" in order to advance. This can work, but you need to pay careful attention to planning for health benefits and retirement since you may not spend enough time at one place to fully "vest" in the company's retirement plan. Your benefits need to be "portable" so that you can maintain the same health insurance and manage your own savings for retirement.

Increasingly, workers are focusing on IRA and 401K plans for their retirement, rather than assuming that they will qualify for a pension. For those employed in a profession, there are professional organizations offering "portable benefits" plans that offer a solution to this problem. Be aware that job-hopping can cause you to have reduced vacation time since you won't always be able to carry-over your seniority from previous jobs. Sometimes increased vacation time can be negotiated before taking a new job.

There are many good reasons to consider job-hopping besides that of seeking a higher salary. It's a good way to learn new skills, expand your network, shorten your commute, or perhaps work from home. It's also a way to escape corporate cultures that are not a good fit for you.

Years ago, many employers were turned off if your resume showed a lot of job-hopping. Today there is growing acceptance of it, as long as you're not changing jobs too frequently. A general rule of thumb is that changing jobs every three or four years is perfectly acceptable. Changing jobs 5 times in 10 years will require you to do some explaining. A history of staying at jobs for less than two years is a red flag for many employers.

If you are working for an organization that you like and want to try to advance, then "climbing the corporate ladder" is the way to go. For some of us, the thought of this may be daunting because it might be too political, too treacherous, or too demanding (and sometimes it is). If you want to give internal advancement a try, there are several things worth paying attention to:

1. **Set a goal.** Figure out what job that you'd like to have and figure out what skills you'll need to be qualified for that job. Seek out the job assignments that will allow you get the qualifications that you need.
2. **Be a team player.** Support your coworkers. Give them credit for their good work, and work hard yourself. Don't be deceitful.
3. **Demonstrate leadership.** Be the person who has a positive attitude and willingness to accept new challenges. Take the time to mentor new employees. **If there are problems, then take the initiative to propose solutions to the problems while being mindful of company politics.** Sometimes the problems are a result of bad management decision that are not likely to be changed. Don't waste your

time or political capital trying to fix problems that were caused by the very people who will decide whether or not to promote you.

4. **Take the time to get to know employees outside of your immediate group.** Build a network both inside and outside of the company. Don't be afraid to let others know about your accomplishments at work.

Whether you decide to stay in your current job, job-hop, or climb the corporate ladder, the fact is that you must take responsibility for your advancement. If you want to advance, then you need to make a plan to achieve your goal.

BROWN

Chapter 8.

So You Want to Start a Company?

Get a grip. Are you **sure** that you want to do this? A common reason people venture into this dark jungle is that they have no idea what they're getting into. Of course a few folks do have a slight understanding of the journey they're about to take, but they are so obsessed with starting their exciting new business that they remain undeterred.

OK, I'll confess that I too have ventured into the dark jungle and been fortunate to have made it out alive and enriched by the experience.

Lemonade
- 50¢ -

FOUNDER

JONNY HAWKINS

CartoonStock.com

Why Start a Company?

There are many reasons driving people to start new businesses. Many want the freedom to "be their own boss." Some see it as a path to wealth and recognition. Others aspire to do unconventional work that doesn't fit into a "typical" business. Some have radically new ideas that require a new business to bring them to life. There also are those who realize that, in their current job, they are not sharing in the wealth being generated by their creativity. Starting a new business where you are the owner solves many of these aspirations Unfortunately, it also brings many big challenges.

The odds of entrepreneurial success are slim. The Small Business Administration estimates that about 90% of new start-up businesses fail within 10 years, with 50% going under within the first 5 years. **Starting a new business is a risky move!**

The reasons for failure are varied but most of the time it's because the money runs out before the sales revenue materializes, the partnerships don't work, or bad market research leads the business astray. I know this from my experiences in start-up failures as well as in start-up successes.

I observed my scientific colleagues take one of two approaches when starting their companies. The first way was "modest": those operating in a garage or small office had a tightly focused technology, bootstrap financing, kept their staffing and operating costs to a minimum, and were driven by a persistent desire to bring this new stuff to the world. The other approach was "glitzy": they worked on raising large amounts of investment capital, creating organizations that had beautiful, well-staffed, and well-equipped offices and a well-oiled public relations department. While the majority of both of these new businesses failed, the "modest" operations had a better survival rate. This was due, in large part, to the persistence of the founders. Those whose aim was to make a "quick-buck" or were beholding to impatient investors failed. Those who were mainly concerned with bringing innovative new products to market and providing good customer service survived.

The lesson here is that success will come to those who are focused on serving the customer's needs rather than trying to simply get wealthy. **Aim for excellence and success will follow.**

What Do You Need to Start Your Business?

All commercial businesses need at least three things:

- a product,
- a customer, and
- a means-to-deliver the product to the customer.

It sounds pretty simple. It's not.

The path to business success is treacherous. Let's consider the new product first. Entrepreneurs always believe that their new product is absolutely great, and if they could only get people to see it, then it would be wildly successful. They subscribe to the old saying, "Build a better mousetrap and the world will beat a path to your door."

It would be great if this saying was true, but surprisingly, most customers are not looking for "a better mousetrap." They might be interested if your new product is lower-cost (but only if it's a lot lower) and if they don't need to change their routine behavior to use it. If your new product is really different and your customers will need to invest time learning how it works and adjusting their routine behaviors then, good luck. New products that change the status-quo only succeed when they offer really significant advantages.

Getting customers is often the hardest part for any new business. Most people don't like to change unless they must. They're usually content to stay with products and vendors that they know, even when they're not completely happy with the product or vendor. Thus it is very important to have specific customers in mind when you are developing the product: They can provide valuable guidance about what they need. They might even be willing to agree to buy your product when you're ready to sell it.

It is not enough to know only generally whom your first customers will be. **You must know the specific name, address and phone number of your likely first customers before you even embark on the new business.** Finding these initial customers can take a long time, months or even years, but you'd be crazy to start a business if you don't know who will buy your product.

The means-to-deliver the new product is always a big challenge. If the product is a service, then you need people to provide the service. But hiring people costs money. You might need a physical space (e.g., an office) where they can provide the service, along with perhaps desks, telephones and office computers. You'll probably want to get insurance for the office space and equipment, and you might need the services of an attorney to incorporate the business. These are just the beginning of the various costs that you are likely to incur before you can open the doors and start generating revenue.

If you're planning to manufacture a product, then the costs get large quickly. You'll need most of the infrastructure of the services business plus manufacturing equipment and raw materials inventory. You could out-source some of the manufacturing operations to save money on capital equipment, but you'll still need specialized equipment to perform final quality acceptance of the products that you'll be shipping.

Whether to Partner

It is common for entrepreneurs to seek and find business partners. Having additional people with complementary skills who are also invested in the success of the enterprise can be pivotal to the success of the business.

Be wary. Choose any business partners very carefully because, as in marriage, you may be together for a long time, and divorce can be devastating. Pay particular attention to these people's integrity (or lack thereof). Remember "your word is your bond" (chapter 2). Your **partner(s) should share this value**, and you can verify whether they do by talking to people who've worked with them in the past.

Every business will eventually experience events that test the integrity of its management. Many partnerships fail because of the devious behavior of an untrustworthy partner.

Pay close attention to whether or not the interests of all of the partners are aligned. If one partner is focused on making a quick buck and the other wants to build a quality organization for the long term, then there will be friction. Alignment of interests is critically important when it comes to financial compensation. If one partner stands to be compensated more (e.g., by virtue of equity position or bonuses) by one business strategy and another partner is highly incentivized to follow a different strategy, then there will be friction. If the financial interests of all of the business managers are not aligned to the same goal, then problems are sure to follow.

How Do You Get Money for the Start-Up?

Basically there are two main paths that most beginning entrepreneurs follow:

1) "bootstrap" financing by the entrepreneur, and
2) financing from outside investors.

"Bootstrap" financing refers to the idea of "pulling yourself up by your bootstraps." The name implies that it is an impossible task, but the truth is it actually can work. In this approach the entrepreneur uses their own money to get started, and then relies on operating revenues to finance the growth of the business. Sometimes the entrepreneur will find additional money in the form of loans from family or friends.

This strategy only works if significant revenue can be generated promptly after startup. As an example, consider a new lawn-care business. If you can afford to buy a lawn mower and a trailer to pull it, then you're ready to start mowing lawns. If you develop a list of prospective customers before buying the mower, then that's even better.

Bootstrap financing does not work if your product requires significant development before you can begin selling it. As an example, only a fabulously wealthy individual could consider a bootstrap start-up of a pharmaceutical company as it takes many years and a lot of highly skilled people to develop new drugs and get them approved for sale.

I have done bootstrap financing of small companies and it worked fine. The downside is that the revenue growth is often slower than it might be in a better capitalized business. Slow growth is not necessarily bad, but you can miss major market opportunities if you are too small and poorly capitalized. So one strategy technology-oriented startups frequently use by is to begin by initially offering engineering R&D services to customers who the entrepreneurs identified before even starting the company. This allows the prompt generation of revenue and buys time to do new product development while slowly acquiring necessary capital equipment. After a few years when the new products are ready, the company's emphasis can slowly shift from R&D services to manufacturing. Bootstrap financing usually allows the entrepreneur to maintain majority ownership and control of the company.

Novice entrepreneurs usually find that getting start-up financing from outside investors is quite complicated and difficult, although this is more achievable if they have a business partner experienced at fundraising from outside investors. Tapping investors for operating capital has the advantage of allowing more rapid expansion of the business, but the downside risks are significant.

To obtain the investment capital, it is often the case that equity (i.e., ownership) in the company is sold to investors. If you've miscalculated the market and your revenues don't ramp up to match the expenses of your new staff, then you burn through the investment money very quickly. Left unchecked, this often results in the investors demanding a larger ownership stake in the company and your loss of a controlling interest. **Investor financing can be a very effective way to start a business, but it can be tricky to manage.**

Finally, it is important to recognize that **the process of introducing new products and generating revenue is not as quick as an entrepreneur might like, so they should plan upon the business having a significant cash-cushion.** In his book "Crossing the Chasm," Geoffrey Moore describes an adoption lifecycle for new technology that does not follow the traditional, smooth "bell-curve" where initial sales are made to early adopters, and then immediately after, to a growing "early majority," followed by significant sales to a "late majority," followed by declining sales to the "laggards". Moore correctly points out that **there is a break in the bell-curve between the "early adopters" and significant sales growth to** the "early majority.". This chasm has been the ruin of many start-ups when the entrepreneurs naively assume that there will be a smooth, continuous growth in revenues.

The reason for the chasm is that time is required for the broader marketplace to evaluate the results that the early adopters are experiencing. It sometimes takes a year or two for third-party reports to be published and absorbed by the marketplace before the sales begin to register. Companies that do not plan for that revenue hiccup are at great risk.

How Much Effort Is Needed?

Starting a business is like starting a family: If you already have a spouse and children, then imagine having a second spouse and a second set of children. The "children" in your business grow from your "brainchild" product ideas. Your business brings you a new "family" of employees, consultants, suppliers and customers. You will know all of these folks on a first-name basis and probably come to know a lot about their personal lives. Most of the business activities occur during the hours of 9 to 5, but not all. The needs of your "business" family will often intrude on the needs of your "real" family, and vice-versa.

Juggling all of this is very stressful. It's only possible if you have the full support of your "real" spouse.

Now You're the Boss. What Do You Do?

As the person who starts the company, you are responsible for everything: figuring out the product strategy; figuring out how to get money; engaging with attorneys, accountants, insurance agents, bankers, customers, and suppliers; and grooming potential employees. You're both the sole employee and the manager. You make the hard decisions, and you get to take out the trash and clean the restrooms.

Once you've gotten the business off the ground and you're satisfied that your business plan might actually work, then **your first major management task is to hire additional staff.** Employees are the most valuable asset in any organization. You can have fabulous ideas, an incredible location, an extensive portfolio of patented inventions and great intellectual property, but nothing happens unless people can translate those things into goods and services that can be sold. Some companies do their best to deny that employees are their most valuable asset so that they can cheat them on fair wages. These are deeply flawed organizations.

Hiring an employee is the single most important task of a manager. Hire the wrong person who is not able to do the job or causes problems for the other employees and you've got a big problem that will be messy to fix. This is especially true in small start-ups where success depends on everyone doing a great job. Hiring a talented, enthusiastic person is essential. How do you find such people?

The traditional method of publishing a "help-wanted" ad, reviewing the resumes that come in, and inviting promising candidates in for an interview can work, but not always. I have had the experience that some folks interview extremely well and turn out to be total duds on the job. Conversely, I've had the experience of provisionally hiring folks who interviewed poorly, but over the long term grew to be the among the best performers in the organization.

Given the unpredictability of the traditional method, we started hiring temporary people from local employment agencies. This allows us to work with the people for a few months to evaluate their skills and see if they are a good fit in the organization. If they don't work out, then we don't renew their temporary employment contract. If they do work out, then we make them a job offer for a permanent position. This approach works very well, especially for non-professional positions. (This strategy is much less useful for hiring professional scientists, engineers and business managers since those folks typically are uninterested in temporary positions.)

When your company gets bigger, you may need to fill a critical senior position in the company. The question that always arises is: "Do we promote from within the organization, or hire someone from the outside?"

128

The correct answer is, of course, "That depends on the people available for promotion." It is often the case that there are people inhouse who are completely capable of being promoted and doing a good job, but they don't get enthusiastic support from others within the organization. It's a case of "the devil you know vs the devil you don't know." The in-house candidate is predictable but often doesn't offer "exciting" new potential. The outside candidate has an incredible resume and references. Hopes run high that they might be able to take the company to enormous success. My advice on this problem is: **Hire the good in-house candidate. You know that they'll do a good job and they've earned it.** Most of the outside hires that I've witnessed failed to meet expectations.

How to Manage People and Earn Their Respect

Managing the people that you've hired is a big job. What's the best way to do this? Do you simply act like a king, issuing commands of what to do and when to do it? Do you scream and yell at employees who are not getting the job done?

These are not the approaches that successful managers use. A wise, highly successful, corporate manager and CEO shared his approach with me many years ago. I have found it to be very effective. This approach is based on five key ideas:

1) **The manager's role is to create the best possible working environment as a servant of the employees.** This includes advocating for better tools and/or work conditions, as well as sheltering employees from corporate drama and distractions.

2) The manager should create a calm environment that doesn't punish errors but encourages people to come forth promptly when errors do occur. Making errors is OK as long as they're not repeated; not reporting errors is unacceptable.

3) **The manager is responsible for clearly communicating what the goals are and what is expected of each individual employee.** The

manager needs to provide a clear understanding of what is exemplary performance and what is unacceptable performance. Providing regular feedback to each employee is important.

4) Effective managers try to guide employees to the correct behavior by engaging with them and asking questions rather than giving orders. Most people don't like to be told what to do.

5) The manager is the "responsible adult" who is expected to arbitrate disputes and make sure that they get resolved promptly and fairly.

Follow those ideas and you'll receive enormous respect as a manager.

How to Manage Expectations

Customers have expectations about the product that they are buying from your business. They expect it to do what you advertise. They expect the product to be safe, delivered on-time and free of defects. They expect you to provide some guarantees.

Investors in your company also have expectations. They expect that you are providing accurate information about the financial performance of the company. They expect that your sales and profitability forecasts are realistic.

The best strategy for managing expectations is to "under-promise and over-deliver." Be conservative, and don't make representations that you are not sure that you can meet. The aim is to prove yourself as **reliable**. Surprises are OK only if they are in a positive direction. Tell the customer that you'll deliver in a week but get it there in 6 days. If you "over-promise and under-deliver" and surprise people with bad news, then you're a bum and you and the company won't succeed.

How to Negotiate

Negotiations are discussions that aim to reach a shared agreement. They are an essential part not only of business, but also of life itself. Every inter-personal transaction involves negotiation. We negotiate with our spouses, families, employers, employees, suppliers, customers, and bankers. Most of the time, these folks are our friends or at least people we respect. It is important to be fair in our negotiations so that we can preserve these relationships. Remember, "friends may come and go, but enemies accumulate."

Good negotiators do their homework before beginning the discussion. They prioritize what they are looking for and (if it is a financial negotiation) the "walk-away" price that they will not exceed. They learn in advance as much as they can about the other party in the negotiation, paying particular attention to what their priorities might be and any issues that might constrain their flexibility.

Successful negotiators maintain a pleasant demeanor and consciously try to listen more than speak. They do their homework and develop specific reasons why their position is justified and fair.

Consider the purchase of an automobile. The first step is to shop around and decide on the specific make, model and accessories. With that information, it's time to do research. If it's a used car you're considering, then examine the "blue-book" values of that vehicle as well as prices from local dealers who are offering the same or similar vehicles for sale. If it's a new car, then go to Consumer Reports and purchase a copy of the "dealer's invoice" for that car. This research will give you an accurate idea of the fair market value of the car. If the car is being sold by a used car dealer or an individual, then you should consider the fair market value to be your "walk-away" price. Offer that much, explaining that it is your "best-and-final offer". If they don't accept that offer, then tell them, "Thank you for your time," and leave. You'll probably get a call back with a counteroffer.

New car dealers need to make a profit on the deal, so it's reasonable in this case to offer a few hundred dollars above the dealer' invoice price. I've never had a dealer refuse such an offer. Is it the absolute lowest price that you could pay? Probably not, but it is a fair deal for both parties. The primary leverage that you have in any negotiation is the possibility that you will not come to agreement and walk away. Never fall in love with the car: You must be willing to walk away if the terms aren't right.

Negotiating a car purchase is a lot simpler than negotiating a complex business deal, but the basic strategy is the same. Do your research. Prioritize the things that are important to you before you begin the negotiation. Learn what you can about the other party and their likely priorities. It is useful to tell the other party at the outset if you have non-negotiable items. Know that it can be strategically better for you to be the first party to put an offer on the table. This effectively "puts a stake in the ground" that is favorable to you. Listen carefully to the other party, and try to figure out how you can meet their needs while also meeting yours. Compromise and creative thinking may be required. If both parties are negotiating "in good faith" (i.e., trying to make the deal work), then an acceptable agreement is often achievable.

There are many good books on negotiation, and it is worth the time to study this skill in more detail. I particularly like the book from Harvard Business School Press "Winning Negotiations That Preserve Relationships."

Plan for Growth

Your company is rolling along. Business is steady. Things are running OK. You're happy with the size of the organization and the workload. You decide that you just want to keep things as they are and enjoy life.

Dream on! Forget about maintaining status quo. Your company can grow, or it can shrink, but it's very difficult to stay the same for any period of time. **If you don't actively try to grow the organization, then the company will definitely decline.**

The rate of growth (or decline) can be managed so that the organization can adjust to the change comfortably, but change is unavoidable and maintaining the status quo is often unachievable. **Plan for growth!**

Thriving On Chaos

Some years ago, bestselling author Tom Peters published a book entitled "Thriving on Chaos" that examined the notion that the world is chaotically changing, rapidly and unpredictably. As a result, the only thing that businesses could expect is constant change, the need for rapid innovation, and a demand for Excellent customer service. These forces are certainly active today. **The solution is to learn to love change and to empower your employees to provide rapid responses to ever-changing customer needs.**

All small businesses are chaotic. Sometimes you're flooded with new work just when your best worker has left for paternity leave. Other times you've just hired new staff and, inexplicably, orders stop coming in. **You don't need to love chaos, but you do need to accept it, or the stress will be your undoing.**

View change as an opportunity. Small businesses are vastly more nimble than larger companies. Your nimble, change-loving organization that provides excellent customer service will be rewarded by repeat customers and a growing business. A few business people actually think that chaos is a comfortable place: Once you're living in chaos, you can't have any more chaos!

Spiral Development, the Path to Successful New Products

New product development is always perilous, especially in a small business with limited resources. You have got to get it right the first time!

A common technique to reduce the uncertainty in product marketing decisions is to do a market analysis based on "voice of the customer." Here, a group of customers is identified to participate in a questionnaire regarding features and benefits that they would like to see in some new product that they might use. Their responses are collated and reviewed to establish a new product specification. The assumption being made is that this process assures market acceptance since this new product specification covers the majority of the needs expressed in the questionnaire. **This assumption is usually wrong. Why?**

The "voice-of-the-customer" questionnaire often can't anticipate other major factors in the new product purchase decision. These factors are only revealed when you've got a prototype of the new product and give it to a prospective customer to try. (The prototype product that you deliver is often referred to as an "alpha" test unit. Once it's delivered to a potential customer to evaluate, it becomes a "beta" test unit.)

Beta testing by the customer invariably reveals items that were overlooked by the questionnaire that are critical to the customer. It takes beta testing with several customers to flush out all of the areas where the new product has failed to satisfy their needs. Only after revising the product design do you have a product that customers might actually buy.

It is also important to understand that meeting 95% of a customer's requirement often does not result in a sale. Customers will buy a new product only if it meets 100% (preferably 110%!) of their requirements.

The product development process doesn't end there. As units are shipped and the number of customers begins to expand, then new requirements will be revealed by enthusiastic customers who want to use it in other applications. This can lead to another round of product upgrades. Thus, **the new product development process follows a spiral trajectory, with each cycle refining the performance of the product to better hit the bullseye of the customer need.**

Assumptions, the Path to Ruin

Most of the failures that I've encountered in business strategy or new product launches have been the result of faulty assumptions. We are forced to make business decisions today to prepare for the business climate in the future. Predicting the future is difficult; nobody has a crystal-ball. If your business is 100 years old, then predicting what conditions will be like for the business in 3 years is not so risky. If you're a new start-up with new technology and only 6 months of sales history, then predicting the future is really just a guess. It is common for the enthusiastic entrepreneurs in a new start-up to make overly optimistic guesses. Assuming that these guesses will become true is a source of great risk.

Sometimes pessimistic guesses are a lot safer. It's OK to be optimistic, but have a plan that accommodates a worst-case scenario without leading to financial ruin.

Assumptions are also the bane of engineering. If your product is complex, then it becomes too expensive to test every element of the design. So invariably, assumptions are made about individual element performance and the design process proceeds based on those assumptions. It is quite common for prototypes to fail because of one or more incorrect assumptions.

The only way to fight this problem is to **always challenge assumptions**: engineering assumptions, business strategy assumptions, marketing assumptions and so on. People who continuously challenge assumptions are regarded as curmudgeons. Do it anyway. **Let your inner curmudgeon out!**

Business Plans and Exit Strategies

Having a business plan is very important. A detailed business plan is absolutely essential if you're thinking about approaching outside investors.

You can prepare a realistic business plan only after you've considered whether you're going to get a partner, and how you're going to finance the business, and develop your product. You need to consider how starting your "new" family (see "How Much Effort Is Needed?") is going to financially affect your "real" family. You need to forecast the expenses that you expect to incur and the revenues that you can expect to realize.

Sometimes the numbers just don't work. You need too much money and can't figure how the revenues are going to cover the expenses. If the numbers do work, then make the plan as realistic as possible since unrealistic projections are only going to hurt you.

One often overlooked aspect of business planning is consideration of your exit strategy. How are you going to get out of this business? Are you going to run it until you die and let your estate figure out what to do with it? Are you aiming to "go-public" with an IPO? Are you planning to hire your kids and turn the company over to them when you retire? Are you aiming to sell the company to a larger corporation?

There are many options. Having at least a preliminary plan is valuable to guide day-to-day business decisions that will support your exit.

Be the Boss When It Comes to Hiring and Managing Contractors

You may be the boss of your own business or not, but what holds true of all of us is that **we have periodic needs for professionals who can provide specialized services for things that we can't do ourselves.** Whether it's a computer programmer, a graphic designer, or a building/remodeling contractor, the process is basically the same.

We'll use building/remodeling contractors for this example. We all have horror stories to share about a botched roof repair or a car repair rip-off. How do we protect ourselves from unscrupulous contractors? Many contractors are honest people but have widely varying abilities. Small, one- or two-person firms tend to be the least expensive, but they might be at the limits of their skills, so quality could suffer if it's not a simple project. Additionally, unforeseen problems that they encounter on other jobs may prevent them from beginning and completing your job. Larger firms have access to a broader range of skills and can usually handle more complex projects. They are slightly more likely to begin and complete the work on schedule. Larger firms generally charge more for their work.

There a several important rules to observe that will greatly improve your odds of success when hiring and managing contractors:

1) **Do your homework, Part I:** *Define the job.* The biggest blunder that most people make is not clearly and completely defining the work that needs to be done before contacting the contractor. Don't speak to a contractor until you've thought the whole project through. You need to be able to tell the contractor specifically when you'd like the work to begin and end, your quality expectations and what work they need to do. It's also important to establish a budget for the project. Some rudimentary internet searches may provide rough guidance on what the project might cost. Google can get you quickly into the ballpark price range. If you're getting a new roof, then just type in something like "average roofing cost per square foot." Keep in mind that these costs can vary considerably depending on your location. This will help you to assess whether the contractor's bid is reasonable or not. **Failure to clearly define the scope of work and quality expectations at the beginning of a project is the single biggest cause of unhappy outcomes.**

If you provide vague guidance to the contractor when they prepare the bid and you accept it, then you are a sitting duck for big cost increases resulting from the "change-orders" that you make in the middle of the job. Contractors are mainly focused on getting the job. Once you're invested in using them, they can cause you grief when they "modify" their starting and completion dates (unless you've stipulated cost incentives related to schedule slippage in the original bid, which is not common on small projects). Change-orders resulting from your poorly defined project scope are cash-candy for most contractors.

Remember too, that "most people are threes." The contractor needs to hear your plan the first time to decide if they will bid on it; a second time so that they can review details to prepare the bid; and a third time at the start of the work as to what needs to be done. If the contractor is hearing three different stories, then you're headed for problems. Get your story straight and stick to it.

2) **Do your homework, Part II:** *Find a contractor.* Once you've established the scope of the job, then ask your friends, co-workers, neighbors and business associates if they know any contractors who

do that work and if they can recommend them. Some contractors are crooks. **It is risky to hire a contractor without a recommendation from someone that you know and trust.** Build a list of the recommended contractors and examine their reviews (if available) on the internet. Call the local builders association to see if they're members and are known to be appropriately licensed, bonded and insured. Call the local Better Business Bureau to see if they've got a lot of complaints. Aim to reduce your list to two or three contractors that you would consider for the project.

3) **Get more than one bid.** Contact the contractors on your short-list and ask them for a cost estimate. Confirm that they are licensed, bonded and insured. Ask them about their current workload and if they can begin work soon. Inquire if they have any local references that you can contact. The conversation will reveal their level of interest and enthusiasm for the job. When you meet with them to discuss the project, you'll get an idea about their punctuality and professionalism. The bid that you receive will reveal their attention to detail. **If you get a bid that doesn't break out the specific tasks that you are requesting and just provides a bottom-line cost, then beware.** They're not really listening to you.

4) **Select the contractor.** Based on recommendations, reviews and the bids that you receive, pick a winner. The best choice is not necessarily the contractor who offered you the lowest price for the project. If all the bids are beyond the costs that you budgeted, then have a conversation with the contractor that you prefer about ways to reduce the cost. There may be some simple changes to the project that can save a lot of money.

5) **Manage the work.** It's a pain, but you need to keep a close eye on the work that the contractor is doing. Try to be present, at least briefly, every day that the work is being done to inspect what they're doing, ask questions about any problems they're having, to praise the work (if it's good) and to point out things that you really don't like. **Your frequent and routine presence will reinforce the idea that the work is important and that you care about it.** If there are

delays, then call the contractor regularly for a status update. They'll get tired of your calls and move you up in priority.

This may all seem very arduous. It is, but following a hands-on "boss" approach will give you better odds that the work will be done properly, on time and on budget. Plus, you'll have found a trusted contractor you can use on future projects.

What Can Possibly Go Wrong?

Most small business owners would agree that if they had a choice between being really skilled or being lucky, that they'd pick lucky. There are so many ways to fail. A devastating fire or tornado, a lawsuit, death or resignation of key employees: Any of these can easily push a small business out of business. Small businesses can "drown in a sea of opportunity," when their product has broad application but the company can't focus on one that generates sustainable revenue. Sometimes a new product launch, like the field-goal kick in football, is "just-wide" and fails to hit the market "sweet spot" needed to be successful. All that you can do is learn from your mistakes and wait for the next opportunity.

There are ruthless competitors who will attempt to steal your ideas, spread misinformation about your company, and try to poach your employees. It's a jungle out there! (Not to mention foreign spies looking to steal US technology...)

What can you do about these risks? For potential calamities like fires, thefts, storm damage, and injury lawsuits, make sure that the business is adequately insured. There are a couple of ways to deal with competitive threats. If you are a technology-based company, then file for patent protection on your technology whenever possible. Your patent portfolio will add significant value to the company if you ever decide to sell it. Fundamentally, the best way to deal with any form of competition is to offer good products at good prices with good customer support. If you position your company to do that, then growth and profitability are within reach.

How Do I Know If My Business Is Successful?

This seems like a silly question but when you're in the middle of running a business, it's sometimes hard to tell. You need to evaluate your success (or lack thereof) periodically so that you can decide whether you want to continue.

There are several different obvious indicators of success:

- You are still in business and able to pay your bills, or
- You are seeing growth in your sales and profitability, or
- You are getting offers to buy your company at an attractive price.

Likewise, there are other obvious indicators that the end is near:

- Your workload is damaging your health and/or family life, or
- Every payday is a struggle to meet the payroll, or
- You're accumulating debt that you don't think you can repay, or
- A new competitor has emerged with a vastly superior product.

In those situations, it might be better to cut your losses and fold up the tent. **Persistence is a virtue, but not when it's clearly going to ruin you.** Besides, enduring a business failure is a common experience of entrepreneurs and one of the best teachers. Use the knowledge from that experience to increase the probability of success in the next endeavor.

Chapter 9.

Some Closing Thoughts

If Things Go Wrong, then Be a Pilot

Things don't always go according to plan: An unexpected situation could have you looking into the face of failure or even physical danger. What do you do when that happens? Pilots are trained to do a 180° turn when things get squirrely. It's a good strategy you can use it too. **Reverse direction and head for a spot where you are not in danger.** The key is to be decisive. Don't hesitate; listen to your inner voice.

When things don't feel right, your situational awareness needs to inform an immediate decision. Continue forward or turn around? It's better to do a 180° turn and reconsider the situation from a distance rather than continuing on to the point of no return.

Civic Responsibility

We are very fortunate to live in a democracy. Our right to vote for our leaders is fundamentally important. Voting is essential to sustaining a democracy and it confers a solemn duty to each citizen to cast their vote in every election. A significant percentage of us regard voting as pointless, and so do not vote. This is a dangerous dereliction of civic responsibility that undermines our democracy.

Today, our political candidates are usually selected from those who enjoy extensive media coverage (e.g., athletes, movie stars, billionaires and career politicians). We pay a lot of attention to their physical attractiveness, their celebrity friends, their party affiliation and their rhetoric that might pander to what we want to hear. Because the selection process has degenerated into a popularity contest, we pay less attention to the more-important questions of their integrity, history of public service and demonstrated leadership skills.

Selecting leaders takes effort from each of us. We must take the time to actually listen to what each candidate is saying and to carefully evaluate their credentials. Do they have experience building consensus between opposing groups? Do they place the interests of the community and country above their own? Are they honest? These basic job requirements cannot be ignored.

In your lifetime, it is unlikely that you will ever find a political candidate with whom you can agree with completely. Nevertheless, it is your duty to support whoever is the best option available; the candidate whose core values best align with your own, and whose skills can best serve the needs of your community. There's never a perfect match, which many folks use as an excuse not to vote. That's just lazy.

Invest in our democracy. Examine the candidates carefully; don't just vote the straight ticket of a particular party. Ignore the pandering blowhards. Choose the best candidates and cast your vote. Encourage others to do the same. It's important.

Consider Burning Man and the 10 Principles

What is "Burning Man"? It borrows a concept from the 16th century Swiss tradition of the **Sechseläuten** Spring festival, that served to herald the arrival of spring, accompanied by burning a tall "Böögg" strawman in the town square.

The present-day Burning Man event was started in 1986 by two guys (Larry Harvey and Jerry James) who decided to build a wooden human effigy and burn it on a beach in San Francisco. Since then, the event has grown in size. Today, Burning Man is held in late August on the playa near Gerlach, Nevada. The U.S. Bureau of Land Management limits event attendance to around 70,000 people.

Getting event tickets is difficult: About half the tickets are allocated to folks who previously attended and are volunteers to support some aspect of the event. The remaining 35,000 tickets are available for purchase on-line at a specific date and time. These tickets are sold-out in a few minutes after they become available.

It's difficult to describe the Burning Man event. The single adjective that I can offer is "insane." It's not a music event. There is no specific entertainment provided (although the whole thing is extraordinarily entertaining). It's a rejuvenating escape from the "default world." It's a spontaneous, experimental community that appears for a week every year and then disappears. The attendees are an eclectic, very interesting bunch; most are quite skilled and distinguished in their "default-world" trades and professions.

The welcoming community is focused on art, self-expression and self-reliance. There is nothing on the playa except a flat, dusty, expanse of land, and you must be completely self-reliant for the week-long event. You must take in all of your food, water and shelter, and leave with all of your waste. There can be no trace of the event left on the playa when the Burners go home.

The "insanity" comes from the scale of the event and the thousands of extraordinary art projects and activities that are erected in a few short weeks prior to the event. If you attend for the week, you'd be lucky to see half of what's there. Some of the architectural art installations are more than 10 stories tall. Most are burned down before the event ends.

Black Rock City (as it is called) is arranged in circular rings and contains all of the camps and art installations at the event. The center ring is 1 mile in diameter. It is surrounded by another dozen or so rings extending out to about 2 miles diameter. Each ring is populated by hundreds of different theme camps of folks who share common interests. I enjoyed the Alternative Energy Zone where generators were not permitted and only alternative energy sources (e.g., solar) were accepted. The city also operates its own airport (FAA designation: 88NV) that handles more flight operations than Las Vegas International Airport. It was enormous fun working as a volunteer to assist in handling the people and airplanes who came and went for the week. When the event ends, the city and airport are totally removed, leaving the playa in its original condition. You need to see it to believe it.

Not long after the Burning Man event started to grow in size, the organizers developed a set of "10 Principles" to guide the activities. To quote from the Burning Man organization:

"The 10 Principles were crafted as a reflection of the Burning Man community's ethos and culture as it had organically developed since the event's inception.

Radical Inclusion
Anyone may be a part of Burning Man. We welcome and respect the stranger. No prerequisites exist for participation in our community.

Gifting
Burning Man is devoted to acts of gift giving. The value of a gift is unconditional. Gifting does not contemplate a return or an exchange for something of equal value.

Decommodification
In order to preserve the spirit of gifting, our community seeks to create social environments that are unmediated by commercial sponsorships, transactions, or advertising. We stand ready to protect our culture from such exploitation. We resist the substitution of consumption for participatory experience.

Radical Self-reliance
Burning Man encourages the individual to discover, exercise and rely on their inner resources.

Radical Self-expression
Radical self-expression arises from the unique gifts of the individual. No one other than the individual or a collaborating group can determine its content. It is offered as a gift to others. In this spirit, the giver should respect the rights and liberties of the recipient.

Communal Effort
Our community values creative cooperation and collaboration. We strive to produce, promote and protect social networks, public spaces, works of art, and methods of communication that support such interaction.

Civic Responsibility
We value civil society. Community members who organize events should assume responsibility for public welfare and endeavor to communicate civic responsibilities to participants. They must also assume responsibility for conducting events in accordance with local, state and federal laws.

Leaving No Trace
Our community respects the environment. We are committed to leaving no physical trace of our activities wherever we gather. We clean up after ourselves and endeavor, whenever possible, to leave such places in a better state than when we found them.

Participation
Our community is committed to a radically participatory ethic. We believe that transformative change, whether in the individual or in society, can occur only through the medium of deeply personal participation. We achieve being through doing. Everyone is invited to work. Everyone is invited to play. We make the world real through actions that open the heart.

Immediacy

Immediate experience is, in many ways, the most important touch-stone of value in our culture. We seek to overcome barriers that stand between us and a recognition of our inner selves, the reality of those around us, participation in society, and contact with a natural world exceeding human powers. No idea can substitute for this experience."

Wow! **Any activity that embraces those guiding principles is guaranteed to offer experiences that are very different from those in the "default-world" that we live most of the time.**

If those 10 principles resonate with you and you'd like to experience something off-the-charts wild and rejuvenating, then consider doing a burn. It will be an unforgettable experience.

Important Laws to Recognize

We are surrounded by laws. Our government creates a vast array of laws that define our legal system and our associated responsibilities for every-thing from paying taxes to driving our cars. Science has brought us to an understanding of a vast array of physical laws, such as the pull of gravity, the speed of light, and conservation of energy and matter, that govern the physical world that we live in.

And then there are laws that aren't physical or legal, but they seem to be always true. Here are a few important ones that you will inevitably encounter:

A) Murphy's Law
   "If anything can go wrong, it will."

B) Murphy's Law Corollaries
   1) Nothing is as easy as it looks.
   2) Everything takes longer than you think.

3) If there is a possibility of several things going wrong, then the one that will cause the most damage is the thing that goes wrong.
4) It's impossible to make anything foolproof because fools are so ingenious.
5) Mother nature is a bitch.

C) The Iron Triangle
Good. Fast. Cheap. Pick any two. The reason being:
- You can do things that are good and do them fast, but they won't be cheap.
- You can do things fast and cheaply, but they won't be good.
(And so on.)
(*There is no way to get around this law. It always applies.*)

D) Pareto's Law (The 20/80 Law)
"80% of the consequences come from 20% of the causes."
So:
- 80% of the sales come from 20% of the customers.
- 80% of the cost comes from 20% of the components.
(And so on.)

E) Issawi's Law of the Conservation of Evil
The total amount of evil in any system remains a constant. Hence any decrease in one direction—for instance, a reduction in poverty or unemployment—is accompanied by an increase in another, e.g., crime or air pollution.

F) Canada Bill Jones Motto
A Smith & Wesson beats four aces.

G) The Peter Principle
"In any hierarchical organization, people tend to rise to their level of incompetence."

H) Hank's Heuristic

"The probability of failure increases with the square of the number of people on the team." (I.e., *Do it yourself.*)

"EVERYTHING IN YOUR LIFE HAS GONE SMOOTHLY. THAT'S A VIOLATION OF MURPHY'S LAW."

CartoonStock.com

Prepare for a Future Run by Computers

We are living at the threshold of a world that is completely controlled by computers. Computers are part of almost everything that we interact with on a daily basis: cars, trains, planes, telephones, toasters, traffic lights, farm tractors, water supplies, power grid, etc. Increasingly, we're seeing manual work being replaced by robots.

These trends are accelerating. The ever-increasing computational power of computers have brought us to the point where the fidelity of digital simulations of the sights and sounds they can deliver are indistinguishable from those that we experience in "real" life. Today, it is conceivable that full-length movies could be made without a single human actor being photographed (imagine Pixar on steroids taken to the next level). Such a movie could star long-gone personalities like Elvis, and we wouldn't be able to tell that it wasn't "real."

This has profound implications. **In a world where digitally created images and sounds are indistinguishable from "real", we lose the ability to use images and sound as proof of "actual" events involving "real" people.** What would we use to verify the authenticity of anything? DNA provides a solution for identifying living things, but how could we authenticate their actions if sounds and pictures could all be fake?

This scenario provides only a mere hint of how our world can get really weird, really fast. The field of Artificial Intelligence ("AI") has been around since the 1950's when the modern computer age erupted. The present-day availability of huge amounts of digitized information combined with more than 70 years of development of sophisticated algorithms by a growing number of brilliant programmers has placed us at another threshold: machine superintelligence. AI machines can currently out-perform humans at a number of games. At some point in the not-too-distant future, AI computers will have the ability to surpass human intelligence at more significant specialized tasks such as pharmaceutical drug development or stock trading.

My own experiences with AI spanned several decades while I was developing miniature chemical sensors that could detect and measure a variety of toxic chemical vapors. The goal was to make an "electronic nose" by using an array of different sensors and analyzing their "fingerprint" patterns of signal responses using neural nets and other pattern recognition algorithms to determine if a hazardous gas was present. The AI technology worked well and could identify patterns more accurately and faster than a human, thereby providing automatic, real-time warnings. The work resulted in a variety of commercially successful products that were used in national security applications. This early experience from 25 years ago gave me a first-hand sense of the power of AI.

This kind of power has grown exponentially in recent years. Nick Bostrom, a well-known scientist and the Director of the Future of Humanity Institute at Oxford University, has carefully considered the impact of AI on mankind. His book, "Superintelligence: Paths, Dangers, Strategies," lays out a sobering set of possibilities that could result when "human level machine intelligence" (HLMI) is achieved. (Most experts have no doubt that it will be achieved in this century.)

Bostrom defines "superintelligence" as "any intellect that greatly exceeds the cognitive performance of humans in virtually all domains of interest." Imagine machines that can do most of what humans can do but 1,000 times faster, or machines that can simultaneously handle 1,000 times more information than the average human. These machines could cause major upheaval in the world, with the elimination of millions of jobs or the creation of extremely powerful business monopolies or military powers.

The primary dangers arise from uncertainty about how quickly this superintelligence evolves. Since the self-learning AI machines are essentially teaching themselves, we might not be able to adequately control how fast they learn. Slow evolution permits better control and allows our political and cultural systems time to adapt and respond. If a self-learning AI machine suddenly "discovers" the algorithm for superintelligence, then the evolution could occur in a very short period of time. Some refer to this as an "AI singularity." The world would be utterly unprepared to deal with this new entity, and whoever/whatever controlled it would have immense power.

My point here is that **you should be aware that this will probably happen in your lifetime, and it is worth supporting initiatives that try to develop ethical guidelines and oversight of self-learning AI machine development.** It may all seem very "wonky" as of this writing, but superintelligent machines could easily be just as significant and dangerous to humankind as the development of the nuclear bomb.

We Are All Ignorant

Would any of us make the ridiculous claim that we personally know everything? Of course not! We can all agree that it is impossible for one human being to know everything. In spite of this recognition, many of us believe that we know vastly more than we actually do know. We take limited experiences and extrapolate them to broad generalizations. We take existing stereotypes and accept them as facts. When confronted with new questions, we allow our imaginations to fill in the "holes" in our actual knowledge to provide plausible answers. We easily become ultracrepidarians without even realizing it, expressing opinions on matters that we really know nothing about. The situation is exacerbated by the vast sea of mis-information, half-truths and lies that we swim in everyday when we surf the web. The world is now full of self-deceived people who think we know a lot about everything and see no need to listen to anyone else We are not the slightest bit inclined to question the validity of our ignorance-based beliefs.

In 1984, the best-selling author, educator, and librarian Daniel J. Boorstin was interviewed in "The Washington Post" where he was quoted as saying **"the greatest enemy of knowledge is not ignorance, it is the illusion of knowledge."** We cannot be lazy when we examine the facts that are the foundation for our deeply-held beliefs. Keep an open mind. Listen to all sides. Avoid just going along with the crowd. Dig a little deeper. Recognize that we could be misinformed. Most issues are complex and are not accurately characterized by black-and-white descriptions. Above all, **we should not be stubborn in our ignorance.**

The World as We Knew It has Ended

The world today is changing rapidly: the climate, the growing influence of artificial intelligence in our daily lives, vast amounts of information pollution, increasing geo-political unrest, the emergence of new diseases, etc. Compared to previous centuries, the rate of change that we are experiencing in the 21st is beyond anything that mankind has experienced. It's not obvious that humans can keep up with this rapid change. Will the machines take over? Have they already taken over?

This is the new world with which you, the younger generation (than me), must deal. **But don't worry: You've got this. Your clear-headed core**

values and preparation will allow you to navigate these challenges. You will do the right things. People like you will lead the world to its future.

Malcom X once said, "The future belongs to those who can prepare themselves today." I think he was right about that. It is my hope that the advice offered in the preceding chapters will be helpful in your preparation for the journey.

Bibliography

Chapter 2

William F. Lynch. *Images of Hope: Imagination as Healer of the Hopeless*, Mentor-Omega Books, New American Library, 1965.

Henry Petrowski. *Success Through Failure: The Paradox of Design*, Princeton University Press, 2006.

Chapter 3

Michael Shermer. *The Believing Brain: From Ghosts and Gods to Politics and Conspiracies—How We Construct Beliefs and Reinforce Them as Truths*, St. Martin's Griffin, 2011.

Yuval Noah Harari. *Sapiens: A Brief History of Humankind*, HarperCollins, 2015.

P. Hübl. "How Conspiracy Theorists Get the Scientific Method Wrong," *Elephant in the Lab* 2020, https://doi.org/10.5281/zenodo.3964396.

Chapter 5

William Strunk & E. B. White. *The Elements of Style*, fourth edition, Needham Heights MA: Allyn & Bacon, 2000.

Lizzie Post, Daniel Post Senning. *Emily Post's Etiquette: Manners for Today*, 19th edition, Harper Collins, 2017.

Judith Martin. *Minding Miss Manners: In an Era of Fake Etiquette*, Andrews McMeel, 2020.

Dale Carnegie. *How to Win Friends and Influence People*, Simon and Schuster, 1964.

"Thomas Jones Quotes." Quotes.net. STANDS4 LLC, 2022. Web: 11 Jan. 2022. https://www.quotes.net/quote/14575.

Chapter 6

Gerard J. Andrews. *Common Cents: Getting Off the Financial Roller Coaster*, Zenjo Press, 2009.

Jack A. Spigarelli. *Crisis Preparedness Handbook: A Comprehensive Guide to Home Storage and Physical Survival*, 2nd ed., Cross Current Publishing, 2002.

J. Alton & A. A. Alton. *Alton's Antibiotics and Infectious Disease: The Layman's Guide to Available Antibacterials in Austere Settings*, Alton First Aid, LLC, 2018.

J. Alton & A. A. Alton. *The Survival Medicine Handbook: A Guide for When Medical Help Is Not On the Way*, 2nd ed., Doom and Bloom, LLC, 2013.

Samuel Glasstone, ed. *Effects of Nuclear Weapons*, U.S. Gov't Printing Office, 1964.

Cresson H. Kearney. *Nuclear War Survival Skills*, New York: Skyhorse Publishing, 1986.

"Yellowstone Supervolcano Eruption History," https://www.usgs.gov/volcanoes/yellowstone/summary-eruption-history

R. Buckminster Fuller. *Utopia or Oblivion: The Prospects for Humanity*, New York, Overlook Press, 1969.

"Design Guidance for Shelters and Safe Rooms", *FEMA Risk Management Series,* Document 453, May 2006.

BIBLIOGRAPHY

Chapter 8

Winning Negotiations That Preserve Relationships, Harvard Business School Press, 2004.

Geoffrey A. Moore. *Crossing the Chasm: Marketing and Selling Disruptive Products to Mainstream Customers*, HarperCollins, 2002.

Tom Peters. *Thriving on Chaos: Handbook for the Management Revolution*, Harper & Row, 1988.

Chapter 9

Arthur Bloch. *Murphy's Law (and other reasons why things go wrong!)*, Price/Stern/Sloan, 1977.

Thomas L. Martin, Jr. *Malice in Blunderland (a foolproof guide for the aspiring bureaucrat)*, McGraw-Hill, 1980.

Nick Bostrom. *Superintelligence: Paths, Dangers, Strategies*, Oxford University Press, 2014.

www.ingramcontent.com/pod-product-compliance
Lightning Source LLC
Chambersburg PA
CBHW071855020426
42331CB00010B/2532